Introduction

Walking through the fire!

The world is becoming a very crazy and unstable place. What used to be one way is now another. It can be hard to keep up with how fast society is changing. In this country, it appears that everything is under attack. What used to be the norm, is no longer anything close to the norm. Some love it, and some are feeling overwhelmed. It is my opinion (I think I'm still allowed to have an opinion in this country—not really sure anymore) that the direction our nation is heading does not have a pleasant ending. This perspective comes from the law-enforcement side of me. This book is my attempt to open people's eyes to see what a cop's life can be like on any given day.

Monday morning quarterbacks—I know we all do this to some extent, but just how far out of control has it become? I will try to explain. Let's take the Olympics for example. How many of us watch the gymnast and find ourselves, in our living rooms, deducting points? Really, what do you know about this sport besides what the commentators are telling you? When was the last time you're out of shape backside ran around the block? Nevertheless, you try to judge a well trained and disciplined athlete? I mean, the next day we go to work talking about gymnastics as if we had competed in the past Olympics. Not all of us, but most do. The point I'm trying to make is that we are used to critiquing whatever we see on the daily news channel. We do it from sporting events to political events—most of which we have zero experience with. We've never played a down or ran for any public office in our lives, but still, we promote ourselves as experts. Note—If you've never voted; don't EVER critique what any politician is doing. Your opinion doesn't count! This brings me to the subject at hand. Have any of you wondering just what it's really like being a cop—not the stories you hear on tv but in real life?

I worked as a complaints deputy for a little over a year along with other assignments during my twenty plus years as a cop. Here, I've included a couple of very interesting questions that I was often asked during that year. I think cops just take these for granted.

How come I see cop cars screaming down the road with lights and sirens on, only to shut them off and pull into a restaurant? Good question. Here's what you didn't see. The cop was more than likely going to a hot call and got called off because more than enough cops had already arrived on the scene. At this point, the cop has no authority to continue using his lights and siren. So, he turns them off and pulls into a restaurant. I can tell you from experience, this has happened to me many times. Most likely, that cop has been running from call to call and is hungry. He now realizes, by the day he's having, if he's going to eat—it better be now. Hence, when he gets pulled off his emergency; he's desperately looking for a bathroom or a place to get something to eat. It may look like he used his lights to go to the restaurant, but supervisors will rip him a new orifice when a cop is caught doing something stupid like that. Yep, do that and get caught; you're going home for a few days without pay, and you can't use your sick or vacation time either.

Here is another often asked question. How come cops drive so fast and ride on my bumper? This is another wonderful question. Let's say a cop gets a call to service stating that a woman hears something out back of her home. She thinks someone may be trying to break in. Here are the keywords that the dispatchers must ascertain. Is it a <u>definite</u> or a <u>possibility</u>? If it's a <u>definite</u>, the cop can use lights and sirens while going to the call. If it's a possibility, the cop is supposed to obey all traffic laws while going to the call. One is an emergency, and the other is an unknown. For, many unknowns turn into nothing. Therefore, the unknown is treated differently. I would ask the person asking me that question, "Just how would you want that cop to respond to your house for the unknown if it was your wife calling—not your neighbor's home but your home?"

They usually responded, "I want him to get there as fast as possible. It's my home."

Well, that is what the cop is trying to do. He is trying his best to get to the call as fast as possible without the use of his lights and sirens. So, maybe just pulling over and letting him go might be beneficial for someone. Then, there's the case where the cop sees someone driving like a butt-head up in front of you, so he's trying to sneak up on that driver to catch him in the act. Cops know if they put their lights on to make you move over, the Butt-head will see this and either turn off the road quickly or just slow down before the cop can measure him with his radar. You moving over just might keep something bad from happening.

Most cops that are directing traffic, greatly appreciate it when they motion for you to stop—that you STOP, and not see how close you can get to them before you stop. That's because when four thousand pounds are coming at you—makes even *Robocop* sweat. Just try to picture yourself out there, with nothing to protect you, while a vehicle is coming toward you, and you have no idea what's going on in that person's mind! Maybe, they're distracted while speaking on the phone. It could be that they're late for something and thinking about all the ways they can try and get around you without stopping. Just because I can see the car, doesn't mean the driver is going to comply, unless the driver stops where I motion him to stop and not where he thinks he should stop. This type of incidence usually makes the cops yell at you. The only supervisors who get upset over this complaint are the ones who haven't directed traffic in a long time. Yep, the office life has made them forget what it feels like to be run up on the hood of a car.

   I'm always amazed when this happens. A cop will walk into a store and maybe buys a few things while in uniform. It seems that there's always someone in the store, at the time, who feels it's his/her civic duty to approach the cop and make the statement, "Is this what my tax dollars are paying for?" For the people who do this or want to do this or are thinking about doing this; while the cop is looking at you, under his breath, he is calling you every curse word he can think of.

   Yep, and creating new curse words that mankind has never heard. This has personally happened to me. It's the reason that I pass the grocery store and go home first, even if I need a few things from that store. Most likely, the cop is off work and trying to help out his wife by stopping and picking up a few items she needs to finish dinner. But, oh no, Mr./Mrs. Citizen is there to tell you about wasting their tax dollars—not having a clue as to whether you are off duty and on your way home, or at work. But, they don't care. (I wonder just how many of them vote?) The last time this happened to me my response was, "Tell me how much money you make, and I'll tell you who pays the most taxes." Anyway, once or twice of this happening, makes you go home first, and then go back to the same store you just passed on your way home.

Here's a good one. When you see a cop that has pulled someone over on the side of the road, slow down as you pass or move over into the farthest lane. The cop has the lights on and is probably conducting a traffic stop. All cops know you are rooting for the driver in the vehicle not to get a ticket—unless they just cut you off, but going past them at *mock 2* isn't funny. It's downright dangerous! It may seem funny for you at the time; until the cop radios down the road for one of his buddies to stop you. I can, without a doubt, guarantee you, BIG ticket coming, big-ticket coming!

Think natural disasters. If you happen to live in a place like Florida, and a major hurricane is coming through; please do what you're instructed. Should you be asked to leave your home; I can assure you that the police didn't ask you to leave so they could rob you. Again, supervisors will make sure a cop goes to prison for that one. The authorities need you to leave, so the cops don't have to perform dangerous or heroic deeds to try and save your ASS. I've tried to apply some humor to these situations—hoping you get the point.

I hear some of you saying, "I know what it's like to be a cop. I've watched *Cops* on tv." Well, you know part of the story. But, let's see if I can fill in some of the missing blanks by giving you some of my own real-life experiences. Let's begin:

STORY #1

My police agency once had us cops attend training. This particular training was about how to deal with the mentally unstable. There was only one part-time instructor there that was an actual cop. Part-time means that the cop instructor was there for only one day out of the whole week. If I remember correctly, the rest of the instructors were from other professions, plus the homeless themselves. Anyway, you might say to yourself, what difference does that make? Such a wonderful question. Cop 101—you can't get up in front of cops to teach them anything unless you have personally gone through the fire, so to speak. How can you tell me how to stay safe, or speak to individuals in a hostile environment while trying to stay safe, if you have never used the principles, in the real world, that you are trying to teach me? You see, some plays seem truly inspirational on the whiteboard, but get your tail handed to you on the playing field. You know— the ones where the team runs this idiotic play that leaves the fans scratching their heads. Come on folks; you don't honestly think it turned out like that on the whiteboard, do you? So, what we cops want to know from the instructor is, has it worked for some poor sucker already? Plus, we want to know why for a very simple anatomy reason—we want to come home ALIVE at the end of our shift! We've become fond of not ending our shift with any extra holes in us that the good Lord didn't put there. Humm, guinea pig? Correct me if I'm wrong, but isn't that the little animal that always DIES after a week or so in captivity?

Let me try to explain this train of thought. Most of the population has no concept of what cops do. The most important part of our job description is explained with this question: "Are you willing to risk your life for someone other than your family—not someone you love very dearly, but a total stranger that might even be hostile towards you at the very moment your life is required of you?" This part of the job description makes a cop's job like no other profession in the world outside of the military, and the military gets to play by a much safer set of rules, or at least they use to. For God's sake, cops have issued to them a gun and a bulletproof vest. That should tell most of you something! What other profession takes you into Hell's Kitchen every day? Try telling a cop there is no devil and you're likely to hear, "Oh really, I know his brothers and sisters!" More on this latter.

For now—back to the training. During one part of the training, this lawyer (gender doesn't matter for this story) was trying to tell us how to communicate with the mentally deranged, and this new way would keep them and ourselves safe. Oh, really? When the instructor was challenged by some of the cops in attendance (hint—Don't ever get up in front of a group of seasoned cops, without knowing exactly what you're talking about, because cops are known to eat their own) as to just how she (oops) was qualified to make this ascertainment; she responded by stating that she had been out in the field with many cops doing ride-alongs. I could see that this instructor's heart was in the right place. Nevertheless, I had to chime in. I said to the instructor that although ride-alongs let you see first-hand much of what cops do, they do not let you experience the most important thing. Instructors who have never been a cop normally don't like this type of participation; hear again, not all! I continued by saying when a lot of stuff is going on, and some sort of decision is required; it's not your backside that's on the line. At the end of the shift, you can go home, and that's making the assumption the officer didn't get you or him/herself killed. Your job was never on the line at any given time during the shift. You only got to experience, to a degree, what the danger is like. You will never be able to fully appreciate the other aspects of the job unless it's your career on the line that decides whether your son or daughter gets to eat. This part of the equation has a strange way of clouding the decision-making skills of the most competent! Think about having these thoughts go through your mind a few times, day in and day out: "Is what I'm about to do, or not do, say or not say, going to get me or this other person killed? Or, is it just going to be ok, or possibly get me disciplined, fired, or possibly sent to prison?" Now, make that decision in a split second. Come on, I know you can do it.

No wonder cops have high rates of suicide and alcoholism. Try maintaining a marriage with all the crap a cop brings home! Some cops who are reading this may say, "I don't have a problem with bringing my work home with me."

To you, I say, "One, you work in a small town where you probably have part ownership in the local Dunkin Donuts, or two, you are physically at the job but you emotionally checked out a long time ago. You start each day counting down the number of days till retirement. Or, you're praying to survive your shift without getting into trouble; only doing what you absolutely must." Sad but true.

Let me ask you this, "How many of you go to work every day wondering if someone's asinine complaint against you is going to cost you your job? then, we'll discuss the possibility of this <u>getting killed</u> thing on top of it." Some of you may be saying you cops probably deserve the complaints. Well, in all fairness—some maybe, yes. Try to remember that in this job, when someone elicits your service; you go—24 hours a day, 7 days a week, including holidays. However, very often when you arrive—nine times out of ten; there will also be someone else at the same location that doesn't want you to be there. Cops call this a **shit storm.** The cop will make one customer happy and the other one—well, let's say not so happy. The one you made happy gives you the thumbs up and the other files a complaint against you. Dear Lord, there's got to be a better way to feed a family hamburger.

STORY #2

This one begins with a shooting that had taken place the night before. One of the deputies had conducted a traffic stop on a subject. The subject punched the deputy in the face and knocked him down. The subject then reached into his waistband, pulled out a gun, and shot at the deputy. Next, the deputy, who was white, returned fire, striking the subject, who was black. The deputy was also struck during this exchange of gunfire. This all took place in a predominately black community. In the early morning, the Sheriff's Office held a press conference to explain what had transpired just a few hours before. They showed video footage proving that the deputy had not initiated the gunfire. Both deputy and subject recovered from their gunshot wounds.

While the press conference was going on, I received a call to service in that same neighborhood where that shooting had taken place. The service call was concerning a black man who was running around the neighborhood wielding a garden hoe. I was informed that an altercation had started between a father and his son. The altercation got out of control with the son trying to attack the father. The father was not hurt and relayed to the dispatcher that his son was running crazy around the neighborhood with the garden hoe and that he was a little slow in thinking, so to speak. Garden hoe, slow in thinking, tried to attack father with the hoe—Hmmm, three things that shouldn't be together.

As I turned into this housing development where the call of service was generated; I saw a black man walking in my direction carrying what appeared to be a garden hoe. He was about thirty feet from me when I spotted him. He saw me and started to run. I hate when they do that because the suspect has to be chased after in the hot Florida sun. Or for me, being fifty-eight years old with sore knees and back from an overindulgent lifestyle of heavy weight lifting— drive after him! I drove a few feet, and he just stopped running. (*Maybe it's not going to be so bad after all*). I got out of the car and started to walk towards him. He was about twenty feet from me at that point. To get his attention, I called out, "Hey, man!" He turned my way and proceeded to raise the garden hoe over his head while walking towards me. (*Ok, maybe it's not going to be a good day*.) With both my hands stretched out towards the suspect like a cop does when he's trying to stop traffic, I yelled at the top of my lungs, "Whoa, Whoa, Whoa!" He took a few more steps towards me holding the hoe over his head like he was going to try and chop me into pieces. He had a crazy look in his eye. Yes, I said eye. Because one was looking at me and the other—can't tell you. All I know is it wasn't looking at me. Then he just stopped, (*Ok, maybe it's going to be a good day after all*.) and dropped the hoe. (*It's getting better all the time.*) Next, the suspect starts to reach down the front of his pants. (*Dear Lord Jesus, this is turning into a nightmare!*) I drew my weapon; screaming, "STOP, SHOW ME YOUR HANDS, SHOW ME YOUR HANDS!" at the top of my lungs; while he was reaching down the front of his pants. Thank God, he showed his hands, *and then is when a certain part of my anatomy started to unpucker*. I was able to get the suspect under control without hurting him.

Here's an interesting part of this endeavor. While searching the suspect, I discovered what he was reaching for—not a firearm, but one of his testicles which was the size of a small melon. *No exaggeration here; never saw anything like it and don't ever want to again.*

For those who watch *Cops* and for that lawyer instructor—the following is what you didn't see and what you need to personally experience to be able to fully appreciate the situation I was in:

1) Earlier in the day, there was a shooting between a white cop and a black suspect in a predominantly African American neighborhood. Therefore, racial tensions are mounting in the community.
2) Looking for someone who's not in their right mind threatening people with a garden hoe. Keywords here...Not in their right mind!
3) An unstable person comes at you presenting the hoe as a weapon to try and hurt you.
4) An unstable person drops hoe, only to reach down paints like he is going to retrieve a firearm. *News Flash: Bad guys don't carry their guns in holsters. They put them in front of their paints*.
5) Mr. Police Officer has a major decision to make in a split second while thinking about

all the things that could go wrong. Sounds like fun, right?

Here are some of the thoughts that went through my mind as the event unfolded. First, I'm a little agitated that I didn't have time to finish my doughnut. (*I'll let you think about that one for a moment.*) Next, chasing an unstable person on foot while he's wildly wielding a garden hoe; It's Florida man and it's hot! What can I say? I'm a big, older guy who sweats easily. What happens if I get close to him and he turns on me and tries to take my head off? I have to have a plan for this possibility before I start chasing him, because when it happens; it's too late to try and come up with a plan. Now, he's coming at me with this hoe. Shooting will stop him. That's if I don't miss him. Plus, there's this little thing about shot placement.

I will take a second to try and clarify my last statement. For all of you out there that are reading this and thinking, "No problem, just draw your weapon and shoot." Well, it's not exactly that easy. Because your body has this nasty little habit of not following instructions under extreme stress, and I think that an unstable person trying to chop your head off = extreme stress. Yes, all cops train for situations like this, but now the reality of *this ain't no training op* kicks in. Here is when shot placement comes into play. Shooting at stationary paper targets on a gun range will not prepare you for this situation, because this target is moving. So, if you're not fortunate enough to have an agency that provides training while you move with simunition rounds (paintball); you're kind of stuck. Firearm instructors get a little uneasy with people running around the range with live ammunition. I know, I know; from the comfort of your home, it sounds like fun. In reality, it's extremely dangerous. Don't believe me—then the next time you go to your local gun range, tell the instructor that you and a few of your buddies are going to run around the range with live ammo. <u>Let me know how that works out for you.</u>

    Let's assume that your round finds its mark. Does that mean the subject will then stop? It all depends on where the round struck the subject. If it doesn't strike a major organ that causes the body to stop, then the attack is still on. Only now, the subject will be closer to you. <u>Let's see—an unstable person trying to take your head off with a garden hoe, who is now closer to you than a</u>

moment ago. On top of that, he has a bullet hole in him that you put there. These all equal a good chance that it's not going to be your day. Again, for those of you who might say, "Nonsense, the subject has been shot; surely it's going to stop him." Maybe or maybe not, and this I can tell you from my personal experience because I've had the unpleasantry of having been shot. *And yes, it does hurt!* There is about a twenty to thirty-second delay until the body registers what just happened. That's assuming you weren't struck in the brain or heart. Thus, causing you to drop dead immediately. So, just because your subject is shot, doesn't mean the fight is over. Therefore, you had better be prepared to shoot more than once. This is the reason cops are trained to shoot until the threat stops. I hope the last statement explained just why cops don't try and shoot someone in the leg. If not, then let's look at it from another angle. Under this type of stress, the chances of you striking the leg are nil to none. (*Only happens in the movies.*)

The cop is also responsible for where the spent round goes. The bad guy could care less where he is shooting, thus will take any shot. Cops don't have that luxury. So, let's look at the leg shooting thing. For one, if you miss, and there's a high chance of it, then where does that bullet go? It will probably skip off the ground and go through Mrs. Jones's window and strike her. Or, two; you strike the suspect's leg only to have the fast-moving bullet go through it, skip off the ground, going through Mrs. Jones window, and striking her. *Poor Mrs. Jones—she's home minding her own business and finds herself with a new orifice*. Now you know exactly why cops are trained to shoot for center mass. And, please, don't inquire about the hand. *That's also a Hollywood thing*.

A Taser may or may not stop a suspect. Several times, I have personally witnessed a deployed Taser have no effect. Short and sweet—Tasers don't always work.

Running around my patrol car and letting the suspect chase me is also an option. That is if I'm faster than him. *If you've seen me run— not an option.*

Getting back into my patrol car and driving away is also an option. *Albeit, one that would probably land me in prison*.

At this time, I'm comfortable with all the events except when the suspect reached down his pants. What came to my mind while he was reaching down his pants was this: What is he reaching for? Is it a firearm? This is where most criminals carry their firearms. I can't shoot him until I wait to see if he pulls out a firearm. If I wait too long he will have time to get off the first shot. What if his first shot finds its target? Will I be able to respond? We just had a shooting earlier this morning and now a second; what's going to happen with my career? That part about my career—cops are instructed not to let it enter their train of thought during a situation like this. Because it can cause you to not react in time to save your life or the life of another. *Years ago, maybe—but in this political climate, and especially what had transpired a few hours before—good luck with that one.* All of this went through my mind, as I drew my weapon while watching the suspect reach down his pants. Talk about a brain full! Say what you want, but you **never and I mean never**, will know what this feels like unless you experience it first hand. Doing a ride-along and watching this unfold is one thing, but actually being the one responsible for making the decision and its outcome is another.

After I got the suspect under control and began to interview him; it was very clear that he was unstable. <u>No, I'll leave the eye thing alone</u>. The man was all over the place and had no comprehension of what almost transpired. He was clearly in some discomfort from his testicle, as indicated by the way he kept reaching down his pants. <u>Sorry I had to give you that visual again.</u>

I drove off with the man—not arresting him, but taking him to a hospital, because, **clearly,** he needed mental help and not a jail cell. I started to think to myself, I was so close to being *that guy*! What do I mean by *that guy*? *The guy* you don't want to be. *The guy* your instructors keep telling you, "Don't be *that guy*!" Since I have mixed blood in me; this day I would have denied any part of the Caucasian in me if I had shot that individual. While driving off with the suspect, I imagined what the newspaper headlines would have read if I shot the suspect: <u>Two Shootings in One Day</u>. Nope, glad I'm not *that guy*. Oh, and by the way; a bottle of scotch was sounding pretty good right about then.

For the Monday morning armchair quarterback, just how would you have handled the situation? The answer is always, you never know until you come face to face with it. This is the reason why it's so hard to instruct cops. If an instructor hasn't experienced situations like this, then how do you expect me to listen to you? I find it amusing when I hear people say if I was *that guy*, I would not have done that. Nope, if you were *that guy,* you would have done the same thing because <u>you would have been that guy!</u>

I often see people making judgments against something they haven't a clue as to what's really involved. I must say, it gets on my last good nerve. Before you judge something, first try to put yourself in the shoes of the other person. Then, just maybe, you might come to a different conclusion. <u>Naah, forget I said that because we are living in different times now</u>. On to the next one.

STORY #3

This story is completely crazy when you come to think about it! It's been said that hindsight is 20/20, and this incident confirms it. On this particular day, we were looking for a certain gentleman who had multiple warrants on him for failing to appear in court and larceny. We also suspected that he was dealing with crystal meth.

Crystal meth is short for crystal methamphetamine. It is a highly addictive drug and takes its user right into the chambers of hell. Over the years on the job, I have come in contact with many females that are using drugs. I have looked at their driver's license from a few years back and they were beautiful women, but now look like a skeleton clothed in skin. It is heartbreaking to see the negative transformation— talk about Beauty and the Beast. The beauty literally becomes the Beast.

Without being an expert on the subject; I believe chemicals such as drain cleaner, battery acid, antifreeze, and cold remedies are among some of the ingredients used to make crystal meth. For the life of me, upon seeing this list of ingredients, why does anyone want to put crystal meth in their body! It is truly astounding what some people will do to experience a super high. Putting all these chemicals together is an extremely dangerous process. There are many well-known documented cases of crystal meth cookers exploding.

We got a tip that the guy with the outstanding warrants was hiding out in an apartment. When we arrived at the apartment, a certain female, who definitely was a meth user—one look at her confirmed it, told us that her boyfriend was the one we were looking for. She said that he was in the apartment. I guess the saying is true, *hell has no fury like a woman scorned*. News flash—<u>Hey criminals; if you are going to have girlfriends, make sure you don't cheat on them. Because they'll get mad and call the police on you. You got to love it!</u>

She gladly unlocked the door and said we could go inside to look for him. Once inside the apartment, it was clear that this guy had been gathering the ingredients to make crystal meth. Empty Sudafed cartons lay all over the place. However, there is no other evidence that he is making the meth in this apartment; at least that is what we thought. Normally, there would be a toxic chemical smell, or rotten egg sulfur-like stink present when these substances are being cooked;

alerting you to get out of Dodge. On this day, no smells were coming from the apartment, nor anything cooking on the stove in the kitchen.

Two other deputies were on the call with me in search of this well-known, <u>outstanding citizen</u>. We looked throughout the whole place, and there was no sign of him. So, we went outside. The female insisted that he was in the apartment. She said she had just walked out and knew he was inside because the front door was the only entrance. She told us that he didn't know she had called, so there was no reason he would climb out the window in the back. We informed her that one of the deputies was already standing in the back of the apartment anticipating this possibility.

We went back into the house a second time. Then, we heard a noise from the attic. It was not really an attic. It was a crawl space about four feet high. There was just enough space for air-condition ducts to run over the ceiling of the apartment. It was a hot Florida day—about 98° outside. I could only imagine how hot it was in an insulated crawl space in the ceiling.

At this point, all three of us were in the house, because we knew he was up in the attic. The only way out of the attic was through a hatch-door in one of the bedroom's ceiling. The hatch door opening was only about two and a half feet by two and a half feet. All three of us looked at each other to see who's the lucky cop that gets to go up in the attic. So, I said, "I'm 270 pounds, this guy here is 300 pounds, and you're a 150 pounder: <u>guess who gets to go.</u>"

As the smaller deputy started to pull the stairs down to climb up into the attic; it dawned on me that this was not a good situation. I said to him, "What happens if this guy is right there near the opening with a baseball bat in his hand, and as you stick your head up there he plays let's see if I can hit a home run with the deputy's head?" Now, this deputy was a little crazy! He was persistent about going up<u>. Maybe I shouldn't say crazy—just young and enthusiastic.</u>

As he stuck his head in the crawl space I yell out, "A deputy is coming up there, and if anything moves I'll be shooting through the ceiling!"

I scream this, at the top of my lungs, a few more times as the deputy crawled up into the attic.

The guy had been hiding behind some of the insulation. He had to be coaxed to come out of the attic. I was thinking, thank God he didn't try to hurt the deputy as he stuck his head up there, plus it probably would have been a better idea to just wait about an hour until he passed out from the heat. A little later, we joked that we should have just sat and waited until we heard a thud, and then pulled him out.

When the guy came out of the crawl space he was soaking wet and covered with fiberglass insulation. *It's amazing what some people do to try to get away from the police!*

I said to him. "Really! It's 98°out- side, and you go up into an attic that's a least a 120°. Why didn't you just try to escape out the back window?"

He answered, "I knew you would have somebody waiting by the window."

I replied, "*So, this is not your first time doing this is it?*"

Once we got him outside, the exchange between him and the girlfriend was absolutely priceless. He said to her, "How could you call the cops on me?"

She answered him, "You should have thought of that before you slept with that slut."

He answered her, "Baby, you know I love you."

And all of us replied while laughing, "*You sure have a strange way of showing it.*"

Then, this guy went on to tell us that he was cooking crystal meth in the house. He said it was cooking in bottles inside a small red suitcase that we had walk by.

I said to him, "The one that I looked in and tried to figure out what it was?"

And he said, "Yes, that one."

Due to the allegations of crystal meth being on the scene, DEA agents were called out to assess the scene. The agents arrived and put on their special suits and went into the house.

In just a very brief time, they came out of the house and had us cordoned off the whole apartment complex and remove everyone from their home until they could control the situation.

An agent explained to us that this was a new way to cook crystal meth called "Shake and Bake." He went on to say the ingredients were put into water bottles and left to ferment. He said that we were very lucky because two of the bottles looked like they could explode at any time. There were about twelve of those bottles in that little red suitcase. The agent explained that this was a new method for cooking meth and that we would have to receive training about it. He said making meth in bottles eliminated much of the chemical and sulfur smell that cops were trained to identify and then stay away if they were smelled.

That was a sobering experience for all of us. And you wonder why cops are becoming paranoid. Today's bad guy is coming at the cop from all different angles—some through planned violence and in this case, just plain stupidity! What other job has a life-altering experience waiting around each and every corner? By now, you should understand what I mean by life-altering—one minute I'm doing police work, and the next minute, my face was blown off and I sustain chemical burns over 90% of my body.

STORY #4

The next story involves the same female from our crystal meth case. I responded to a grocery store about a female possibly getting ready to steal some items. When I got to the store, the management informed me that their loss prevention agent was watching a female put certain items into her purse. They pointed out the female to me. *Lo and behold, it was my friend from the "Shake and Bake" crystal meth apartment case.*

I was standing at the exit door about twenty-five feet from her. She had a shopping cart full of mostly non-perishable items and a few groceries. She was talking on the phone and saw me when she looked up.

I gave her the cop stare—the look that says, "Hey, I'm the police and I'm watching you."

She looked at me, then looked away, then looked at me again. The whole time, I had my arms folded and looked at her like I knew what she was up to. She became nervous, dropped her phone, and walked away from the full shopping cart.

At that same time, the loss prevention officer caught my attention out of the corner of my eye. She had been trying to hide behind one of the shelves but was not doing a very good job of it. She was short and had to keep jumping up and down to see over the shelf to maintain a visual on the suspected shop-lifter, Mrs. Crystal Meth.

The loss prevention agent came over to me and asked if I would step out of the store, so she could try and catch the girl in the act. <u>I didn't have the heart to tell this young lady that her surveillance methods were not covert.</u> I agreed, thinking this suspected shop-lifter knew who I was and saw me watching her, plus there was no way she was going to try to steal anything, now. So, I stepped out in front of the store and waited. While I was waiting, an FTO (Field Training Officer) showed up with a trainee. He asked if he could have this case because it would be good training for the trainee. I agreed.

A few minutes later, management of the store came out and said they had apprehended the woman and had her in custody. With that, the trainer, trainee, and I went into the loss prevention office to interview my friend, Mrs. Crystal Meth.

The trainee was interviewing the woman who said she did not take anything. The loss prevention agent was accusing her of stealing a Brita Water Filter. She went on to say she observed her put the water filter into her purse. We instructed the female suspect to open her purse. Lo and behold, there was an empty Brita Water Filter box inside her purse. The trainee was not able to get any information out of this seasoned professional criminal.

Then, I jumped in and asked if she remembered me? She answered, "No, should I?"

I reminded her about the incident with her boyfriend and she said, "Oh, that was you!"

I said, "<u>Yes, it was me. I guess the green uniform makes us all look alike.</u>"

I asked her what did she do with the water filter? She told me she did not take any water filter and that she just found an empty box in the bathroom. I told her okay, I'll buy that, but I was going to go into the ladies' room and search every inch of it. And if I found the water filter in the trash, we would charge her with the theft. She looked at me and told me to go ahead and that she didn't care.

With that, I was determined to find the water filter. This girl was not going to play me. I went to my car, got my disposable gloves, and gloved up. I rummaged through the ladies' room garbage—just a footnote here for the men: lookout for used sanitary napkins and tampons. I didn't care. I was determined to find the filter. The more filth I had to go through, the angrier I became! I must say, some of you women out there are just downright disgusting. I found used tampons on the floor— Lord Jesus! The least you ladies could do is put them in the garbage.

I didn't find any water filter, even after going over every inch of the ladies' room. I did find a bunch of other very interesting items, but I'll save that for another story. So, I went back to the office and informed everyone that there was no filter to be found anywhere. We charged her for petty theft because she had walked out of the store with the box in her purse.

I asked the trainer to watch how she walked to the patrol car because I was sure the filter was stuck up between her legs somewhere. We watch her as she walked, and there was nothing odd about the way she moved. She walked absolutely fine. We were dumbfounded because the trainer and I were positive that she had stuffed the filter up her vagina, and that's where she was hiding it. The trainer said they were going to take her to jail anyway, and that she would be searched by a female officer when she got there.

My shift ended, and I went home. About forty-five minutes later I was eating at the dinner table when I got a phone call from the FTO. He was laughing hysterically on the phone. He told me I could never guess where the water filter was.

I said, "So, she did have it. How was she able to walk like that with the filter up vagina?"

The trainer was in tears when he told me they put her on the X-ray machine at the jail, and the water filter was up her anus (*Do you realize just how big a Brita water filter is?*). This woman was only about five feet six inches tall and ninety-five pounds. The FTO went on to say this brings a whole new meaning to someone saying this water taste like shit.

I thanked him for giving me a visual that would take some time to get rid of, and for ruining my dinner.

STORY #5

On this particular day, I received a call to service regarding a woman who had found a little boy running around her backyard. The woman had informed the dispatchers that there was a young boy, who appeared to be about four or five years old, wandering around her backyard. (Race is not important for this story.) I responded to the address and met with the woman. The woman told me that she was watching her little daughter when she saw this little boy running around her backyard. She said she brought the boy into her home and asked him what was his name and where did he live? The boy was able to tell her his name and showed her where he lived. He lived in the home that was behind hers. So, she took the little boy by his hand and walked through her backyard and then through a fenced-in yard. She told me she knocked on the door very loudly but receive no answer. Then, she decided to call 911.

    I asked the woman how long the child had been with her? She told me about forty-five minutes. I asked her to continue to watch the child while I drove around the block to the front of the residence where she said the child lived. I knock on the door. There was no response. I then began to bang loudly on the door, and finally, a woman opened it. I asked this woman if she had a little boy named so and so; as I described the child to her. She told me yes that she has a son fitting the description. I asked her if she knew where her son was? She replied of course, yes. He's in the kitchen eating breakfast. The hour was past lunchtime during this conversation. I then asked her if I may come into her home so she could show me where the child was. She said sure. Both of us walked into the kitchen. A bowl of uneaten cereal was on the table and the back door was wide open. I then told her that her son had been with the neighbor for the past hour. She told me that he must have just wandered off. This woman was clearly on some sort of narcotic and been sleeping and not watching her five-year-old son.

This woman's home had a pool in the backyard that was filled to the top with polluted water. The water was completely black. Also, there was no toddler fence around the pool. The backyard was fenced in. However, once in the backyard, anyone could have fallen into the filthy pool. I asked her about this dangerous situation due to her having a very inquisitive little boy. The woman seemed very indifferent to my observations.

The home was a wreck. Feces was in the bathroom toilet. I was told that the toilet was broken, and the family used the toilet in the unfinished building outback. The little boy's room was completely disgusting. By this time, I want to drop-kick this woman. Times like this make it hard to be a cop. You have to act professionally and disregard your feelings.

The state's child agency was called and came out to do their thing. The result of their investigation was to leave the child with the mother, have her clean the home, get the toilet in working order, and secure the pool.

I filed a warrant for child neglect against the little boy's mother. The warrant was approved, and the little boy's mother was arrested a few days after this event. The arrest happened on my day off. *I would have worked for free on that one.*

The story doesn't stop here. About ten days after this, I got a call to service about a young child that had fallen into a pool. Guess where the call to service was. Yes, you guessed it, at the same address. Now, I remind you, this is only about ten days after I had this woman arrested for child neglect. This time, when I got to the house, my lieutenant had already arrived and had pulled the little boy out of the pool. This precious little boy that had been so full of life the last time I saw him, was now dead. I started to lose control at this point. I don't remember all that happened that day—only parts. I can remember grabbing the child's mother as my lieutenant yelled for me to be professional. Well, his words got to me, because I let go of her. To this day, I'm not sure what I would have done if my lieutenant had not been there. I remember walking across the street and crying my eyes out. Yep, just like a little baby.

That event struck me to a core—as no other had ever done before. You see, being a cop gives you a front-row seat to much of the evil the world has to offer. But, when it's against children, it kind of leaves you empty inside. All I can say is thank God for my lieutenant's presence on that day. God only knows what my response would have been. And yes, justice was served. The little child's mother received jail time. Recalling this event still brings back a hollowness even though it's been years since the incident. Let's move on to the next experience.

STORY #6

I'm 6' 4" tall and I've weighed around 275 pounds for most of my adult life, so I'm not the average type of guy. I can't say I've been afraid of much but big spiders—don't know what they feed these suckers down here in Florida. Then there are roaches—these things look like they came out of a nuclear reactor. They kind of make my skin crawl. One day while driving my patrol car, I had a Mickey D's cheeseburger sitting on the front seat. I had already eaten one. <u>*Ok, let's cut the crap. They were double cheeseburgers, and I had eaten two of*</u>

them. Alright, you feel better now. Anyway, as I was driving, someone must have done some insanely stupid thing right in front of me for me to conduct a traffic stop—especially with an *uneaten, mouth-watering, ketchup oozing, still warm in the wrapper, sweet-smelling Mickey D's, double cheeseburger still on the front seat of my patrol car*. Well, I did the traffic stop. *Sorry Mr. Cheeseburger, daddy will be right back.*

I can't recall what the driver had done, but I was going to write him a citation. Looking back; just what was I thinking? Those who know me, are aware that a strange form of arthritis comes over my fingers when I touch a citation book—can't figure out just what it is, but when I pick up this book; my fingers start to curl up which make it nearly impossible to write. So, I retrieved my citation book and guessed what popped out of the book—a little Cucaracha! It's panic time! At that moment, the book went flying onto the passenger's side floor. Then, oh no—one of Cucaracha's brothers popped out from under Mr. Cheeseburger! With that, Mr. Cheeseburger goes flying out the window, don't know where it landed, and don't care. Now, mind you, as of yet I hadn't made contact with the driver, but was determined that this crazy driver, who had disrupted family bonding time with Mr. Cheeseburger, was going to get a ticket.

Instead, I turned my blue lights off, spun the car around, and headed straight to fleet maintenance. I just left the driver of the other vehicle sitting on the side of the road with no explanation whatsoever. I can't even imagine what went through his mind. I didn't *pass go* but went directly to fleet maintenance in a somewhat urgent way. (That's cop talk for hauled ass.) <u>Dear God, I hope my supervisor is not reading this!</u>

Once at the garage, I jumped out of the vehicle, thinking it had stopped first, and rushed to one of the mechanics. The available mechanic—let's just say is this military guy that had spent much time over-seas; looks at me as if I'm crazy. I try to catch my breath while explaining that there are little monsters in my car.

He said to me, "That's what all this is about."

Then, he starts to laugh at me. Yep, he laughed at me. At that same time, some of the other mechanics started to come over and get into the conversation. Now, I have three guys laughing at me, but you know what—I don't care. All I know is that there are little monsters in my car, and I ain't driving it again! Just in case I wasn't clear, *I AIN'T DRIVING IT AGAIN* until the whole family is gone!! The first mechanic told me that it may have been just a couple of roaches, but he would remove the plate that covers the floor jam to see. I'm standing a few feet away as he removed the plate. Then, all hell broke loss as these horrible little creatures came running out and went all over the place!

Without thinking about it, my hand instinctively went right to my weapon; with him yelling, "Whoa, what are you going to do—shoot them?"

I said, "Sounds like a good idea to me!"

By now, all the mechanics are laughing hysterically at me—you think I care?

One of the mechanics said to me, "Such a big guy and afraid of a little roach."

First of all, it's not just a little roach. It's the whole neighborhood! I drove a spare vehicle for the next few days until they got the roach motel under control. For those of you who may be inquisitive as to how the roaches got there in the first place—have you ever examined the caliber of people who visit the back seats of a police car?.. this brings me to my next experience.

STORY #7

I answered a call to service about two teenagers not wanting to go to school. Yes, at times, cops do the truant officer and parenting thing with other folks' children. *I still haven't figured out why, but we do.* So, I arrived at an apartment with this mother telling me how her children were refusing to go to school. Her son looked to be about eleven and the daughter about twelve years of age. Both children sat on the sofa while I spoke to them about the importance of school attendance.

As I was speaking to them, these horrible little creatures started to run from behind the sofa and up the wall. Some ran this way and the others ran that way. It's day time, and these things are running around the wall like they own the place! One, then two, then three, back and forth, up the wall, and down the wall. I started to wonder if I was the only one seeing them. Maybe I had been traumatized by those creatures that had hijacked my patrol car. The mother didn't say anything to me about the roaches. *Surely she could see them—right. Someone, please tell me she can see the roaches!* This went on for about ten minutes. I didn't want to say anything, because—well, you know—trying to be professional. (*Oh, dear Lord, I'm trying so hard.*) I mean, how many roaches are there since they aren't concealing themselves when the room is all lit up with sunshine streaming through the windows? For anyone who is not familiar with these things—God bless you. But, for us who do not have them in our homes, and have to daily go into the homes of other folks who play cards with them—makes your skin crawl.

Not to get off point, but I once responded to an apartment at night, and when the homeowner turned on the lights; the whole wall moved*! I ain't lying*! The whole wall was covered with roaches. When the lights came on they all went scurrying, and so did my behind; right out the front door—*tripping and falling flat on my face*. I wasn't the least bit embarrassed, either.

Let's get back to the original story. I started talking to the mother because the kids were ignoring me. As I talked with her, one of the roaches jumped off the ceiling and landed right smack in my face! Yes, on my right cheek. It had to have been a cousin of one of the roaches that had been on Mr. Cheeseburger. You may ask me, "How do you remember it was your right cheek?" <u>Really</u>, one can't forget a traumatic event like that. I didn't jump six feet into the air. Still, to this day, I don't know how I stayed calm. I slowly removed my glasses and brushed my cheek—acting like *Robocop*. All the while I was **freaking out Inside.**

Right now, I want all of you to stop for a moment and close your eyes. Now, picture being in a room with roaches running all around you, and then they start to JUMP ON YOU!!! <u>Now you're getting it!</u>

I'm now ready to get some gasoline and burn down the building. Is that an exaggeration? <u>Yes. No. Maybe.</u> When the mother saw me brush the roach off my face; she said in an ever so polite voice, "Oh, I'm so sorry." <u>Lady, you're sorry—now, you're sorry? Why didn't you tell me Godzilla was getting ready to skydive onto my face?</u>

Well, this call to service is over. *Kids, you can go to school or not. I don't care anymore.* Once the mother and I were O-U-T-S-I-D-E, I shifted the conversation by suggesting a field trip to Home Depot to buy some bug bombs might just be what the doctor ordered!

Have you ever witnessed a dog frantically rolling around in the grass? *I now know that grass stains don't wash out of a polyester uniform so easily*. You can't even imagine what it was like driving around in my patrol car for the following few hours. All I could think about was one of the roaches might have been Houdini and was still camping out on me. Thus, those damn little monsters were coming back. A job at UPS was starting to look *pretty good* right about that time! On to the next experience.

STORY #8

This experience was rather interesting; something that definitely catches a cop off-guard; until you've done the job for quite some time. Then, nothing seems to surprise you anymore. It was around 2:30 a.m. on a Saturday. My work assignment area for that night was close to the next town which has a few nightclubs. On Friday and Saturday nights, young people frequently use the highway, that runs through our county, as a drag strip. Therefore, a cop will position himself out there and just wait to see what the night brings his way.

On this particular night, a BMW came speeding down the highway. The speed limit on the highway is 45 mph. My radar measured the BMW at 60 mph. Cops usually set their radar for about 10 to 15 mph over the speed limit, and that is the speed at which they will begin to stop vehicles. This all depends on the cop. So, I conducted a traffic stop on the BMW. Little did I know that the show was about to begin!

I approached the driver's side of the car. As the driver rolled down the window, the smell of alcohol punched me in the face. There were three females in the car and all appeared to be young. This was a small convertible type BMW. Two of the three young females were sitting upfront, and the other one was sitting in the back. The girl sitting in the back began to laugh and say some crazy things. Clearly, this girl was not intoxicated but inebriated.

The passenger sitting up front began laughing along with the girl in the back; the two of them expressing that this is the funniest thing in the world. They started to call me the Popo, a slang term for the police. Then, they proceed to tell the driver that she was going to get a ticket and that they think this is the funniest thing in the world. The passenger sitting upfront is also inebriated.

I asked the driver for her driver's license, registration, and proof of insurance. She tried to retrieve them. While she was looking for them, she began to explain what was going on. She said they had just come from a bar, and she was the designated driver. She continued by saying she had not had anything to drink, and that she could imagine how bad this looked. I told her not only does it look bad, but it doesn't smell too good, either. She then told her friends to shut up. After she said that, they laid into her harder. The one in the back started making fun of the driver by saying that her boyfriend was going to have to bail her out of jail. The girl in the back continued to ramble on while slurring her words, all the while laughing very hard. The passenger sitting up front continued laughing and saying she thinks this is the funniest thing in the world.

Now, the driver was having a hard time finding her driver's license. She started to panic a little bit and told me, "I know I have them." At this point, the girl in the back goes into hysterics—seeing that her friend can't find her driver's license.

The girl in the back said, "Why don't you just show the cop your boobs if you can't find your driver's license. That's what I always do."

The minute I hear that I said inside of myself, "*This is about to get stupid—really, really stupid.*

About that time, the deputy working close by; responded to assist with my traffic stop. This is something cops normally do for each other—especially late at night. That's because, if something is going to go bad, two are always better than one. He walked up to the back passenger side of the BMW and became aware of what was transpiring. (*Thank God, I don't have to go through this one alone*). Clearly, at a time like this, a female partner would have been a whole lot better. Let me try to explain.

When a male cop pulls over a female who is batting her eyes at him and trying to show him some skin; if the male cop doesn't give her a ticket—see where I'm going with this. If he gives her a ticket, then he is the cruelest, heartless bastard in her eyes. However, when a male cop gets into a situation like this and he happens to have a female zone partner, then he can pass the traffic stop off to her. When the female driver finds out that now a female cop will be conducting this traffic stop instead of the male—well, the expression on the female driver's face is priceless—simply priceless.

Now, the girl in the back said, "If you won't show him your boobs; I will." And with that, she pulled down the top of her dress and exposed her breast—*two very large breasts, I must say*. She continued to laugh hysterically while shaking her breast all around the back seat of the car.

When the driver saw the girl in the back, she also began to laugh as she told her friend in the back to cover up. The girl in the front passenger seat was also laughing at the one in the back seat. It could be seen that the brain cells of the girl in the back seat had already deteriorated due to alcohol consumption.

By this time, the whole fiasco had been going on for about five to eight minutes. Then, the driver found her driver's license, but then dropped them between her seat and the front console. The driver then asked me if she could get her driver's license for me. I told her, by all means. At that point, she opened the driver-side door and bent over, looking down between the seat and the console.

This young lady was wearing an extremely short skirt. When she bent over, looking for her driver's license, her skirt began to disappear into thin air. I saw that she was wearing nothing but Colgate Dental Floss. As she was trying to find her driver's license, I think it dawned on her that her backside was completely exposed. She began trying to pull her skirt down. But as short as the skirt was, it wasn't covering much of anything, even when she was standing up. While she was trying to pull her skirt down, I wanted to say to her, "_Good luck with that one._" But I resisted. It was very hard for me to keep my mouth shut on that one. She searched around for about a minute before she finally retrieved her driver's license.

I had the young lady driver walk with me to the side of the road. There, I began to interview her. The other deputy kept watching the *Howard Stern Show* back at the car. As I spoke with the driver, it became clear that she had told the truth and had not been drinking, and that she was the designated driver. She went on to apologize for her friends' behavior. I asked her if the girl in the back seat always behaved like this.

She answered, "Well, not this bad." Now, this is where cops can get into trouble for saying what I said to her. I asked her if she was aware that when she bent over she had completely exposed herself to me? She said she wasn't aware of it at first, but when she reached around and grabbed her skirt; she became aware of it, but what was she to do?

I said, "Maybe wear longer skirts, especially if the Popo is going to pull you over. Or, how about not purposely dropping your driver's license between your seat and console when you wear only a dinner napkin and dental floss."

She went on to tell me she didn't purposely drop it. I then explained to her that her friend in the back seat could be arrested for exposing herself. She told me that she was so embarrassed that her friend had done that, but that it was kind of funny. She went on to tell me that I must be old because all the young girls dress like this now. <u>I thought this is exactly the reason young couples should pray to have only boys.</u>

Then, the other deputy walked over to me and said, "I've seen enough, so I'm out of here."

I said to him, "You're not leaving me alone here with this sideshow." With that, I gave the young lady back her driver's license and told her to slow down.

Some may be thinking to yourself, "Why didn't you just give the driver a ticket, and arrest the girl in the back seat for indecent exposure?" If I had done that, I can almost guarantee you that the following scenario would have transpired.

The one who got arrested for the indecent exposure would have hired a lawyer. I am sure the lawyer would have tried to turn the situation around to make it look like I did something wrong.

To corroborate the arrested girl's story, the other two girls would have to jump on the side of the girl who got arrested. I'm sure, with the testimony of the other deputy, I would be able to beat this.

However, here's the problem. When a complaint is made against a cop, even though the complaint is unfounded, a record remains in the cop's file that a complaint was made against him/her. If a cop gets two or three complaints of the same nature, even though they're unfounded, people begin looking at you as if you're circumventing the situation. The general public looks at a cop's file and sees he/she has had complaints made against him/her. They don't care that the complaints were proven to be false. In this day and age, false complaints do add up, and the general public knows this. In the past, if a cop wasn't getting any complaints, the supervisor called him/her into the office and chewed him/her out. The supervisor would say, you clearly aren't doing any police work, because no one has complained about you. Today, cops are more afraid of the complaints than getting into a gunfight—sad but true. My, have the tables turned.

STORY #9

My sergeant and I responding to a call to service where a drunk guy was harassing one of his neighbors. The guy was very intoxicated, and I believe he had pushed the other neighbor. The drunk man became very combative as we were trying to restrain him. My sergeant and I finally got him into handcuffs. Then, we proceeded to drag the drunk to my patrol car, with him struggling all the way. This guy was about fifty plus years of age, Caucasian, 5' 9" tall, and about 230 pounds. He was so drunk that he could not walk alone. While dragging the man to my vehicle, he committed the cardinal sin! Any cop who has dealt with this before will know exactly what I mean. The guy was so drunk that he produced one of the worst cases of diarrhea that any human being could ever experience. Yep, his light-colored shorts turned dark brown in a matter of seconds. To top it off, the feces began running down both of his legs.

At that moment, my sergeant let go of the drunk and started to laugh while saying to me, "Guess who's going to have a pleasant ride to the county jail."

I said, "_Really sarge, really? Are you going to leave a brother hanging like this?_"

His answer was, "Absolutely, you don't think he's going to get in my car, do you?"

With that, I proceeded to uncuff this individual as my sergeant asked, "What are you doing? This guy has to go to jail."

I reply, "_Just what did he do again?_"

Laughing, the sarge said, "Good try, now take your prisoner to jail. " The funny part here is that as my sergeant and I were having this conversation, this guy stopped being combative and just stood next to my patrol car listening to everything.

Then, this drunk white guy chimed in with a drunken smile on his face slurring his words, and said, "Yeaaa sargeeee, ssshow the brrrrother some love."

When he said that both my sergeant and I simultaneously said to him, "Shut up!"

I remembered that we had trainees working that day. I called to see if one of them needed an arrest for training purposes.

Then, the sergeant said to me, "Good luck with that one! But what the heck, it might work."

So, I call for one of the trainers to see if their trainee needed an arrest for training purposes.

One trainer said, "Yes, we're right around the corner and we'll take it."

I looked at the sergeant and said, "_Well, what do you think of that?_"

He replied, "We'll see."

After about a minute the FTO pulled up. The deputy and his trainee got out of their car and started walking toward us. I tried to position the drunk so that the back of his paints did not face the FTO and his trainee as they walked up. During this whole time, this drunk guy seemed to be enjoying all the attention. He just stood there, swaying back and forth, saying nothing. The FTO got about four feet from me, and the drunk guy let the rest of his cocktail breakfast out. Yep, big old juicy, gurgling one. Fresh feces started to run down his leg. The FTO saw the mess and yelled for his trainee to get back into the car. He didn't say it nicely but raised his voice. Then he drove off very deliberately (hauled ass).

By this time my sergeant was in tears from laughing so hard,(<u>No really, he was crying</u>) and at the same time saying to me, "How'd that work out for you while gasping for air?"

For the cops out there—don't you just hate your supervisors at times? Oh, and yes—the thought of quitting right there on the spot did cross my mind.

With that, I turned to the drunk guy and said, "Really, dude."

Then, he just smiled at me and let out another fart.

I forcefully put the drunk man into my patrol car. I'm only human. I knew that due to his high alcohol consumption, I would first have to take him to the hospital before jail. My patrol car sat baking in the hot Florida sun while I stayed with the drunk man at the hospital. Afterward, I had to endure the luxury of riding with this drunk to the county jail with my head hanging out the window. If you ever saw a cop drive past you with his head hanging out the window—*you don't have to wonder about that anymore*. I don't recall any discussion of this type of incident at the academy. The recruiters and trainers enticed you with, "Come be all you can be. You'll get to drive fast and use lights and sirens to chase bad guys. You'll make a difference in your community." *Really! Really—this is your description of making a difference—a bunch of liars!*

    This type of situation would be a perfect scenario for a large agency where cops don't take vehicles home. It is referred to as *Hot Sheet*. The vehicle is driven for one shift and then brought back to the station for the next shift to use. The problem with *Hot Sheet* is when one shift causes an issue with the vehicle; they will try to hide it, so the next person who drives the car will take the blame for it. Just imagine not rinsing out the back seat and then parking the car outside in Florida's hot temperatures, and the next guy has to drive it—Beautiful!

    A take-home patrol car is assigned to one cop, so he/she takes full responsibility for it.

I can just imagine that some of you, who are not cops, are reading this and thinking that cops are mean people. For, who would do such a thing to a colleague? Remember, earlier I said cops eat their own. This is one of the examples I'm speaking of. Cops will harshly tease each other when a mistake is made. But, most cops eventually get to know, at least I hope they do; (*Come to think of it, maybe that's why Leroy, Billy, and Savana never came back to pick up their paychecks.*) It's all in good spirit and the laughter releases the misery. Let me try to explain.

Police officers are endued with a peculiar sense of humor early in their careers. This sense of humor becomes a coping mechanism to protect their emotional state of being. Sometimes the horrific situations that cops have to deal with can leave the mightiest of them severely shaken. The average citizen doesn't have a clue as to just how dark this world really is; nor should they. That's why cops do the job, and they keep this darkness from the average citizen. How would you handle arriving on the scene of a suicide where the deceased used a shotgun splattering half of their brains around their bedroom? Or, how about a major traffic fatality on the freeway where little children are involved? Or, the mass shooting where you have to walk through the carnage left behind? Or, the husband and wife who beat each other bloody, day in and out, and every time call for your assistance? Or, the toddlers, and yes, I did say, toddlers—left to fend for themselves, because the mother is addicted to crack cocaine? Should I continue? Now, are you, somewhat, comprehending what some who wear the uniform have to endure?

Since cops constantly deal with these emotionally stressful situations on a day to day basis; the profession teaches them a way of trying to cope. For, you will learn how to cope, or you will quit very early in your career, or you will resort to the bottle, so to speak. Some find the cruel reality of the job too much and stick a gun in their mouth. Depending on where they work, the things some police officers have to deal with can truly be overwhelming at times. I very, very often remember the little boy I got to know and then witnessed his drowning. We all have our *kryptonite*. For me, the splattered brains and body parts are easier to deal with than the abuse of little children—enough said. So, all I ask is that the next time something happens and you see some police offices standing around and maybe laughing; don't automatically assume that they are a bunch of cold hard bastards, for just maybe they feel like crying, but are trying to control their emotions in another way. You do realize that cops are required to maintain complete control throughout all situations. Even though the world is falling apart around them, cops don't have the luxury of expressing their emotions. They must maintain sureness to convey to those around, that everything is going to be ok. This is not an option, but a job requirement.

STORY #10

This incident occurred while working in a part of town that was known to get "a little off the chain" at night. An FTO with his trainee and I were each parked, in our separate patrol cars, behind one of the area schools. It was about 3:00 a.m., and since it was relatively quiet, the FTO was going over some training briefs with his trainee.

Then, we heard what sounded like a few gunshots. We paused, but then all was quiet. We didn't become alarmed since this was a constant occurrence in this particular neighborhood at night. The FTO resumed his instruction.

Then, we heard more gunfire. This time, we get into our patrol cars and headed in the direction of the gunfire. We drove with our windows down so we would be able to hear what was going on. As we drove up the block, we heard a few more and then about ten to fifteen shots in a row. The FTO and his trainee were driving up the street about two car lengths in front of me.

All of a sudden, I saw the FTO make a sharp left turn onto a street. Suddenly his car door flew open. He jumped out, kneeling behind his door, with his weapon drawn, and started shooting at something. I couldn't see what the trainee was doing because it was very dark. At the time, I was still about two car lengths behind.

I slammed on my brakes and pulled over to the side of the road. This thought ran through my mind, "Since they're shooting at someone using their handguns; I should bring a little more firepower to the gunfight."

With that thought, I proceeded to retrieve my shotgun from my patrol car.

Most shotguns are stored on a locked rack behind the front seat up near the roof of a patrol car. If the deputy stored the shotgun this way; to retrieve it, the deputy must first push a button on the door to release the lock, and then and only then can it be pulled out of the rack.

I got my shotgun, all the while hearing a bunch of gunshots going on. I beat myself up in the car while trying to quickly retrieve the shotgun (The human body's response in stressful situations can create challenges). I would have to guess that it took me about five seconds to retrieve the shotgun. With my shotgun in hand, I ran around the corner to where FTO's car was.

Both the FTO and trainee were shooting through the open doors of the patrol vehicle as I approached. I looked down the street in the direction that they were shooting. I saw someone lying on the ground with another person standing over them and shooting at the FTO and trainee. I saw muzzle flashes going off as this subject fired his weapon at us. This subject was about forty yards down the road.

I pointed my shotgun at the subject and proceeded to fire it. **Nothing happened**! Shotguns are carried in patrol vehicles with no round in the chamber and the safety on. It's called curser ready. The deputy must first rack the shotgun to put a cartridge in the chamber. Then, push off the safety to be able to fire it. So, after pulling the trigger and it did not go bang, I remembered—hey Hotshot, you need to rack the damn thing also, and I did.

I racked the shotgun and then the subject stopped shooting at us and ran across the street onto someone's front lawn. I think this guy had one of those Hollywood guns that never needed any reloading, or so it seemed that night. This was taking place on a street that had homes on both sides. I tracked the suspect with the shotgun. Then, I decided not to shoot. Because, one, he stopped shooting at us, and two, he ran in front of someone's home and I couldn't remember if I had a slug in the chamber or regular buckshot.

Knowing the type of ammo in the chamber was important. If it was buckshot, I would have taken the shot, because any buckshot that might have missed the suspect would have been stopped by someone's wall. On the other hand, if it were a slug and I missed—well, little old innocent Mrs. Jones getting shot, while in her bedroom, was a possibility. That slug would have gone through any wall.

Cops are responsible for where their spent rounds go. Shooting back at a subject leaves a cop with no options. If a subject is running away from you, and you don't have a safe shot; don't take it.

Now, let me clarify what had happened. This subject was shooting at another subject who was lying on the ground. That information was relayed to me as I was approaching the scene. Since the suspect had already shot someone and was currently shooting at the police—yes, by all means, the cop is justified in trying to stop the person before he hurt someone else. The situation that the FTO, his trainee, and I were currently in, justified the use of deadly force. Another way to look at this is if the suspect came in contact with someone else in the next minute or so, is there a possibility that this person might inflict bodily harm on that person? The answer here was, yes. This suspect was not afraid of the police and had no regard for anyone's life as demonstrated by his actions. A violent crime was in action; not some other situation. This was a real live gunfight!

    This event taught me some important lessons. It taught me the importance of training and practice. For example, don't try to do anything you're not trained for, and the practice of drawing your weapon and shooting targets on the gun range makes the drawing of your weapon a natural response. Most importantly, <u>not</u> practicing removing your shotgun from your vehicle under stress—well you can see what you get. In my case, I stored my shotgun in the trunk of my patrol car, because I thought it would be easier for me to retrieve it from there. <u>*And, nothing more to say about this*</u>! Oh, and YES, my shotgun fiasco was used in training as a *what not to do* example—damn cops! Now, PLEASE, it's time to move on to my next call to service experience.

STORY #11

This incident took place in the same community where the shooting had occurred. On this night, I was assisting a deputy who was conducting a traffic stop. This deputy had stopped a vehicle for having no tag light. The deputy was an FTO and had a trainee along with him. The deputy was letting the trainee conduct the stop while he observed.

The FTO could smell that something was not right, so he walked up and took over the traffic stop from the trainee. The driver was asked to step out of the vehicle to speak with the FTO. I could see that the driver became extremely nervous. The FTO asked the driver for permission to search the vehicle and the driver said ok.

The FTO had the driver walk to the front of his patrol car which was parked behind the subject's vehicle while the trainee and I search the subject's vehicle. During the search, I found a small bag of marijuana in the vehicle and brought it back to the FTO. Now, please understand; I'm not a drug cop, never have been and never will be. I've never been interested in the whole drug thing.

I was proud of myself for finding some drugs in a vehicle because normally I'm not asked to search. I usually just stand by and watch the subject—which is fine with me. Therefore, I was proud of myself as I gave the bag to the FTO. The FTO looked at the bag and continue to interview the driver. As far as I was concerned, the problem was solved, but nooooo, not for this FTO.

He told me to watch the guy for a moment while he went to search the car. I thought to myself, that's ok with me—don't know what else you're going to find, but go ahead.

After about a minute, the FTO came walking back to me with this large bag of cocaine and said, "What's this?" while holding it up close to me, so that I could see it.

Both the trainee and I had missed the cocaine. I don't know how and I didn't really care now.

The FTO laughed at me and said, "He is a trainee, but you?"

The FTO was a drug cop with many hours of experience that the trainee and I lacked. He had developed superior interviewing skills. The driver's reaction told him that there was more to this than what I had found.

To this day, that deputy doesn't know how close I came to snatching the bag of coke out of his hand and throwing it into the canal. Yep, I thought about it but decided that wouldn't go over too well. So, I got into my patrol car and drove off while saying a few choice words to him as I left.

The many shared experiences like this help form a bond between the men and women who wear the uniform. At times we can be perceived as a big dysfunctional family. However, when troubles roll in; we're right there —ready to do whatever is necessary for one another. This brings me to my next call to service experience.

STORY #12

I stopped my patrol car at a red traffic light at an intersection. There were three lanes of traffic— a turn left only to my left, and two straight forward lanes. I was in the middle straight forward lane. There was one vehicle in front of me, and a vehicle in the left turn lane.

The light switched to a green arrow for the left turn lane. The two straight forward lanes' lights remained on red. With the forward lanes' lights still on red, the vehicle in front of me made a sharp left turn in front of the other vehicle that was ready to make its left turn.

Two white guys were in the vehicle that was about to make the left turn. A black guy was in the vehicle that cut them off. I was sitting right behind the vehicle that illegally cut off the vehicle attempting to make the left turn (got to make you wonder just what some people are thinking). I felt like yelling out the car window, "*Hey, Dummy. Don't you see a cop parked right behind you?*"

The white guy sitting in the passenger's seat was wearing a red ball cap. He pointed to the driver that had just cut them off, turned his ball cap around backward, and spit a huge gob of, I'm guessing, chewing tobacco out the window. The driver began to spin the tires and took off after the black guy. I thought to myself, "Maybe I should act like I never saw a thing and let history take care of itself."—just thinking.

For those who are reading this and want to turn it into a racial thing—I'm BLACK, but stupid is as stupid does. _Read no more into it. Thank you very much!_ However, being a law enforcement officer, I turned on my lights and went after the two of them. Yes, both cars.

The vehicle with the two white guys must have seen me behind them and turned off the street. To this day, I wonder what might have happened if they would have caught up to the other driver.

I caught up to the black driver who had greatly exceeded the speed limit by this time. I pulled him over. Some may ask, "Why did you pull over the black guy?" Humm, let's see. All I had on the two white guys was that they had spun their tires. The black guy made an illegal left turn, deliberately cut in front of another vehicle, drove recklessly—does that answer your question? I've previously acknowledged that I'm the type of cop who doesn't like writing traffic tickets, so my whole purpose was to give this guy a lecture and hope he understood. Right now, some readers may be saying, "Come on man; surely this guy should get a ticket." Well, yes, and no, because every case is different, and only by interviewing the individual is a cop able to decide. So, in this case, did I have someone here who was reckless and didn't care, or was this person preoccupied and not paying attention? But, before you hand me over to the sharks and tell me I'm stupid, consider this.

    I work in an area that has a large senior citizen population. Young people who live here refer to the city as the Stairway to Heaven. Many times, I have witnessed this same type of incident involving senior citizens. My parents raised me to be fair and impartial. So, I take every case on its merit and interview people to see if their action was a faux pas, impatience, or something else. This comes from my character and not the academy. Yes, most of the senior citizens in my area are Caucasian, but doesn't the black driver deserve the same criteria? An important thing you learn as a cop is that things aren't always what they appear to be. For, appearances can be very deceiving, and rushing to judgment can be devastating to the innocent. Hopefully, you can now understand why I used the race of my subjects in this example. Now, on to finish this story.

I approached the driver's window. I asked for his license and other documents. He started to become extremely nervous— face twitching, sweating like a pig. I asked him if he always responds this nervously during a traffic stop? He said that this was normal for him. Then, I asked him to step out of his car. When he got outside of his car, the left side of his face began twitching rapidly. I asked him if he was alright, and he told me he was. This guy was so nervous that I said to him, "Now you're starting to make me nervous, so I'm going to pat you down to make sure that you don't have any weapons on you." The man complied. After the pat-down, I put him in the back seat of my patrol car.

Then, I asked him if he would give me consent to search his vehicle; with him saying that would be ok. I found a backpack in the backseat of his car that contained drugs and a laptop with a picture of him on the home screen.

I arrested the man and charged him with possession of the drugs. To this day, I still don't understand—*Mr. Bad Guy, if you have drugs in your car; don't give the police permission to search*

<u>it. *Do you really think when you tell cops, that it's ok to search, that their response is going to be, "Ok, fellas, let's not search this vehicle because surely there is nothing in it?"*</u>

STORY #13

This experience took place while I was on patrol in my assigned area. Another one of our deputies was in pursuit of a white male driver who supposedly had a large quantity of narcotics in his possession. I don't remember all the details, because it took place in the west of town which was out of my assigned area. I listened in on my patrol car's radio transmissions because it was my agency that was chasing this guy.

At one point in the chase, another one of our deputies put *stop sticks* in the road to try and get the vehicle to run over them to blow out the tires, so the vehicle would have to stop. However, the driver being pursued swerved to miss the *stop sticks* and continued. According to the radio transmission given by the deputy, as the driver swerved to miss the *stop sticks*, he almost ran over the deputy.

Our department deployed its helicopter to assist with the pursuit. Once the helicopter was up and had located the suspect's car, all the other cop's vehicles pull back and let the helicopter track where the subject was going. If I remember correctly, this whole thing went on for about fifteen to twenty minutes. While this type of event is going on, a deputy will still pay attention to it in the background, even if it's not in his area, because he/she still have calls to service to perform in their area.

At one point, the helicopter pilot reported that the subject had just stopped his car and gotten into another vehicle that was waiting for him. The pilot reported that the subject was the passenger in the car and someone else was driving. With the new information, deputies anticipated where this vehicle might show and headed in that direction.

It was reported that the vehicle was heading south on a major highway that ran through my area of responsibility. Therefore, I position myself at an intersection that the subject's vehicle would have to pass if it continued heading south. I faced east at a four-way intersection. Traffic coming from the north and heading south was to my left. I could hear the pilot calling out the subject's vehicle's direction of travel. After a moment, off in the distance, I saw the helicopter flying toward me and still calling out the direction of travel for the subject's vehicle.

Next, the helicopter was about 100 yards from me and flying canted sideways about forty feet off the ground. As I watched the helicopter flying sideways and very low to the ground, I thought that this must be what it's like to be a cop in LA. I mean, I didn't know a helicopter could be flown like that—pretty cool if you ask me. Anyway, the helicopter got closer, but I still couldn't see the vehicle he was describing.

Then, the light turned green for my lane to go and for the traffic heading south, to stop. I asked the pilot to identify the car because the helicopter was not moving but hovering about five car lengths behind the subject's vehicle.

At this point, all the vehicles in front of the subject's vehicle started to pull over and the subject's vehicle started to pull forward. With that,

I pull my car out and block traffic in the southbound lane.

Then, I got out of my car and drew my weapon while yelling for the driver to stop the car. I saw that the driver was a white female with a white male in the passenger's seat. As I walked towards the vehicle with my weapon drawn and yelling commands, the car's wheels started to spin, but the car did not move. I could see that the passenger had part of his body in the driver's seat and was grabbing onto the steering wheel. The female driver was crying while grasping the steering wheel and saying something to the driver.

By this time, all traffic had stopped at the intersection. No vehicles were moving in any direction. I continued to approach the vehicle. Its windows were down, and I could hear the male shouting, "GO, GO, GO!" with the female screaming at him to stop. When I got to the side of the vehicle where the male was sitting, I saw that he had his foot on the gas peddle and the female driver had her foot on the brake. Suddenly a wonderful idea popped into my mind—something within me said, "Shoot the car's tires to end this thing. Right now."

By now, I'm going to guess, that this chase had been going on for about thirty minutes. The suspect had driven at high speeds, ran through intersections, and almost struck a deputy with his car. He had called some female to meet him and was still trying to continue his escape, even though a cop was right there in front of him with a gun pointed in his face. As I was in front of the vehicle, I thought, if that car comes towards me; I will have to jump out of the way because I can't shoot into the car and possibly hurt the female; who I could see didn't want this to go any further.

Well, I didn't shoot at the tires, and I thank the good Lord I didn't, because I would have gotten into *a load of crap* over that one. <u>Yep, I would probably have been asked to turn in my playbook</u>. Instead, I pull open the passenger-side door; while the whole time, this ignoramus was yelling at the female to Go, Go, Go, as he pressed on the gas peddle.

The front of the car was swerving back and forth, but going nowhere as the tires were spinning. I kept my weapon on the suspect because I didn't know if he was armed. I tried to pull him out of the car with one hand. Just as I was attempting to do that, two other deputies came upon the driver's side, and one of them deployed a Taser. With that, we were able to get the jackass out of the car.

While we had this guy on the ground, he said to one of my lieutenants, "You guys are just mad because I made you chase me."

With those remarks, my lieutenant drew back his leg like he was going to knee spike this jackass in the head, but he used self-control and didn't do it. I knew he wanted to though because I could see the *knee spike to the jackass's head* look in his eyes.

I asked the lieutenant what would have happened if I had shot out the suspect's car tires.

He just rolled his eyes and said, "Thank God, you didn't."

We got the whole scene under control and started to get the traffic moving again. There was a yellow Nissan sports car stopped next to the subject's car. A female was in it. It was evident she had been frightened and was visibly shaken from having had a front-row seat to all this chaos.

She very politely asked, "Can I go now?"

Through my experiences over the years, I have come to notice that there is a very big difference between chasing the white guys and the brothers. The brothers will make a few sharp turns and then bail out of the vehicle with the doors open and the car still moving and leave the drugs inside. By the time you catch up to them; there is no one around, just an empty car. The white guys will do their best to try and save the drugs. They flee from you but stay in their vehicles—drugs and all. I guess they're the captains of their ship, so to speak. Therefore, when you finally catch them; you've got them hands down. But, with the brothers, you have to be *Usain Bolt* to catch them in the first place, and if you do—and that's a big IF; they deny ever having been in the car you were chasing. The brothers will be all hot and sweaty and whatever shirt they had on will have already been ditched somewhere. Plus, they may be all cut up from running through bushes, but will still emphatically insist that they were home watching the football game. *You gotta love it!*

STORY #14

I got a call to service where a woman had called stating that someone had stolen two of her television sets. I arrived at the home and was greeted by a woman in her seventies. She told me that she allowed her daughter to live at the residence. She said her daughter had informed her earlier in the day, that someone had stolen the two televisions from the home.

The homeowner went on to say that she had insurance and wanted to file a claim. I asked the mother if anyone had broken into the home and she said she didn't think so. I said to the mother, "Ok if no one broke into the home, just how did the televisions come up missing?" The mother told me to ask her, as she pointed to her daughter.

While interviewing the daughter, it wasn't long before I ascertained that she had a substance abuse problem. The daughter told me she had a party in the home the previous night and that she did not know most of the people that were there.

She went on to say that she had passed out on the sofa and wasn't sure what happened afterward.

After interviewing the daughter, I told the mother I would be happy to take the report, but I asked her if she was sure that she wanted me to file a report of what had transpired in the home the previous night concerning her daughter. I informed the mother that anything the police recorded was for all eyes to see. The mother asked what I meant by that? I let her know that anyone, at any given time, can go to any law-enforcement agency and request reports concerning anyone. I told her it was called the *Sunshine Law*. I told her that if she told her insurance company that her televisions were stolen; for the company to pay; they would first have to see that a crime had been committed. The insurance company would request a copy of the police report to see just what had happened and then determine if they were liable.

The mother said she didn't know that police reports could be read upon request. Then she said, "So, you would report that my drug addict daughter had an orgy here last night and was too stupid to control who she let in my house, and today I'm missing two of my televisions sets?"

I said, "Ma'am, I wasn't going to word it quite like that, but something to that degree."

The woman got up from the table where we were sitting and said, "Oh, Hell No. I don't want anyone to know just how stupid my daughter is."

And with that, she looked at her daughter and said, "I guess if you want to watch tv you'll have to go and buy one."

Then she thanked me for my time.

STORY #15

On this call to service, I conducted a traffic stop on a young black male (race is important here). The male was a big eighteen-year-old lad. He appeared very studious and wore a pair of black rim glasses that had white athletic tape holding them together. The young man told me that he was on his way to the local college, and that was why he was speeding. He was very polite. I asked him if he paid for his insurance. He told me no his father paid for it.

It is my practice, that anytime I stopped a young person for speeding while driving a vehicle and they don't pay for the insurance; I have them call one of their parents. I also do this for those who are underage and living with their parents. My reason for doing this is when I give the young driver a ticket; I'm penalizing the parent because they are the ones who have to pay the enormous insurance premiums. Hence, I do what I would want someone to do for me if they stopped my child.

I told to the young man to get his father on the phone.

The kid looked at me big-eyed and said, "What?"

I told him that he had heard me tell him to call his father because I wanted to speak to him.

He said, "What for?"

I reiterated for him to just get his father on the phone. The kid asked if there was any way for me not to do this?

There, I saw something going on that I didn't see very often in my profession—a child that was very concerned about what a parent knew about his actions. About half of the young adults laugh at me when I ask this of them, and they usually just say ok. The reaction I saw from this young lad told me that his father was going to take care of business when he got home.

The young lad finally called his dad. He explained to his dad that he had been pulled over by the sheriff's office (Most kids would have said the cops.) and that the deputy wanted to speak with him.

He gave me the phone. I introduce myself and ask to whom was I speaking? The father yelled at me and said I already knew who I was speaking to, and just why the hell did I stop his son? I started to think maybe this was a bad idea because this might be one of those parents that thinks their child can do no wrong. I began to explain why I had stopped his son. I informed him that his son was going twenty miles over the speed limit. Then I gave the dad my little spiel about not wanting to penalize the parent, and asked if I could trust that he would take care of this issue so that I wouldn't have to write his son a citation?

The father apologized for being a little abrupt and asked me to please put his son back on the phone. I handed the phone back to the son.

I stood about four feet away from the son and heard the father yell into the phone, "PARK THE CAR. PARK THE CAR AND WALK HOME!"

The son asked the dad if he knew where he was?

And the father yelled into the phone, "I don't care if you're in Fucking Africa! Park the car and walk home!"

The kid pulled the car over into a nearby parking lot and removed all of his books. Now, I felt really bad for the kid. I asked him where he lived and he told Sebastian. This traffic stop took place near Interstate 95 and Sebastian was about 15 miles away. I asked him if he wanted me to drive him halfway there? He told me no; he would just walk because his father would probably call and meet him halfway.

I guess this dad was no joke! Now, that incident reminded me of something my dad would have done—*old school.*

STORY #16

This call to service had me running radar on a major highway that runs through the county. I measure a car going 65 in a 45-mph zone. As soon as the car passed me, I pulled out and drove in behind it. Both the speeding driver and I had to stop for a red light. I was sitting directly behind the car that I was going to stop.

Well, I guess the driver thought he would pull the, *I will just pull into this store parking lot, jump out of my car, and run inside*, move. Yep, people try it all the time. I think the train of thought is, if I park really quickly and get out of my car, the officer won't know it was me driving. Folks, cops see this move all the time, and we laugh to ourselves as we pull behind you and order you back into your car. This guy pulled into a bank parking lot and got out of his car really quick. He starting walking fast—almost running into the bank.

I drove up to the front door of the bank and cut him off. I had my window down and told him that I would be right there when he came out.

The young man stopped and said, "You got me."

I had him go back over to his car and asked him just what was he thinking? He was a young black male who shrugged his shoulders and told me that he didn't know.

I said to him, "Let me guess; your licensed is suspended, right?"

He asked me how did you know?

I said, "Can I ask you a question? You don't think you're the first one to try that little maneuver, do you?"

I found out that the vehicle he was driving belonged to his grandmother with whom he was living. The vehicle's registration had expired and his license had been suspended for not paying some tickets. However, he said he did have insurance on the vehicle—*Ok, one out of three*; not bad. He went on to say that he was in a hurry to get to a temporary job interview. He was nineteen years old and said he needed the job to help pay some of the bills for his grandmother who he lived with.

So, I proceeded to give him the lecture: If you had not been speeding I would not have a reason to stop you in the first place. Then, I told him that he should be arrested for driving on a suspended license, plus his grandmother's car would be towed. Also, he was probably looking at a few hundred dollars in fines plus the towing fee. I asked him where his job interview was and he told me it was right up the street.

Finally, I told him I would let him go if he would promise to start driving like he had some sense and get this taken care of. He said thank you and we parted ways.

About a year later, I saw this young man at Sam's Club. He walked up to me with his Sam's shirt on and asked if I was a cop? And I asked him why was he asking? He told me that he thought I was the cop that stopped him and gave him a break. When I knew he wasn't some crazy guy that was going to go off on me in the store, (*Yes, that happens sometimes*), I told him I was a deputy.

He told his co-workers he knew it—that I was a cop.

He said, "You don't remember me, do you?"

Then he proceeded to remind me about the event, and I told him that I remembered. He told me he got a good job. He said that he not only got his driver's license back but he also finished paying off his grandmother's car and got its registration. He said thank you so very much and then proceeded to tell all the Sam's Club employees what a great cop I was.

Whether you want to believe this or not, most of the veteran cops that I have had the privilege to work with, say this is what this job is about.

That was one example of what I mean by the importance of taking time, with each encounter, to ask questions to find out if you have someone who needs some help, or if it's just someone who is trying to get away with something. At times, it can be hard to tell the difference. Nonetheless, it is time well spent. With my next experience, I didn't do a very good job with the interview.

STORY #17

This night's assignment had me working in the north part of town. It was about 3:00 a.m. and not much was going on. I had to make a pit stop. (Pit stop means cop having to go to the bathroom; yep— number 2).

Having home-field advantage does have its perks. That's why many of us cops like to work in the area where we live—when nature calls; you're on home turf. I am a little squeamish about using strange bathrooms—you've either got this problem or not. Earlier that night I had gone to Mickey Ds. Cops that work at night eat at fast-food restaurants most of the time. Later on, I decided to give Mr. Cheeseburger a break and grabbed something at one of the convenience stores instead. I can hear a lot of you cops out there saying, "*You're going to be sorry*." Yep, I was sorry alright! My belly started to do the gurgling thing. The only problem—I'm almost 8 miles from my home. Again— I got this little squeamish thing going on.

Let's digress from this account and have a moment of silence for all female cops. Why? For male cops, half of their "nature callings" can be rectified with just a quick zip of the paints. For female cops, it's like getting dressed (duty belt—

gun, holster, ammo pouch, radio, etc.) for the start of their shift at each "nature calls."

Back to that assignment night. So, I call my zone partner and advised him of what I was going to do—hey, man it's 3:00 a.m. What could go wrong, right? I boogied home—cop talk for 'hauled ass'. Then I boogied back.

On my way back, a vehicle up ahead of me came across the grass median and began heading south in the northbound lanes! The vehicle was coming directly at me! I was driving, let's just say, a tad over the speed limit—a behavior that definitely brings on early labor for cops' supervisors. I'm thinking, "*Come on vehicle, you can stop! Oh, baby, I know you can stop for Papa.*" I stopped! Thank the good Lord I had already gone to the bathroom—wouldn't have been pretty. Adrenaline was pumping through my veins, due to the drunk driver almost broad-siding me.

The wayward driver's vehicle had stopped sideways, blocking both lanes of northbound travel. He had been heading south before he lost control and came into the northbound lanes.

Thank God, it was 3:00 a.m. and not earlier in the day.

The driver was extremely intoxicated— drunker than a skunk. I got him out of the vehicle, and he could hardly stand up. However, he was very polite—not the usual drunk. The driver offered no excuses and said that he deserved to go to jail.

Therefore, I took him off to jail. He called his wife from jail. When the wife arrived at the jail, she asked to speak with me. I was prepared for the usual responses that arresting officers normally hear—he's not a bad guy, the dog ate his homework, and so on. However, she was very somber. She told me that he had some type of cancer and that he had but a few weeks to live. Also, she said that she thought he may have been trying to kill himself.

I felt like a horse's ass. I asked the man why he had not explained what was going on in his life. He said that he deserved to be there in jail and it was not my fault, because I was only doing my job.

I went to the court on the man's court date and explained to the judge what had happened. The judge dropped his DUI and had him attend a program to help with his emotional problems. A cop's job is not easy to always get it right. Take away being human and it becomes much easier.

At times, I have given back-up support to other deputies that are conducting traffic stops. On occasion, I have heard things said that I disagree with. I speak up when that happens.

Let me explain. When I hear a deputy ask someone if they can search their car, and the person says ok—I'm dumbfounded. Hey, Dude, the United States Government has just asked if they can search your property.

It's my practice to tell people, "You know, you can say no, don't you?"

I'm amazed at how many people don't know their constitutional rights.

This is completely mind-blowing to me because I was raised in a family of law enforcement officers and lawyers. The purpose of defense attorneys was drilled into me. It was put this way, take that away and you better pray to God you or your family don't find yourself on the other side of the law. Each member of my family was instructed; if a cop ever approaches you and asks if they can have a word with you, the response is this, "Can this lead to me or any other family member getting into trouble?" If the answer is yes—LAWYER!

The questions that cops ask need to be relevant to the nature of the traffic stop. Cops can't just assume there is something wrong. We must have some sort of stink that leads us down the trail, and not, "I just think this guy is dirty".

I have personally witnessed some cops trying to do something, and I have had to remind them that we can't do that. I have interrupted cops interviewing people on a traffic stop and told the people being interviewed that they should know they don't have to answer.

I would explain Miranda to people like this: *You have a constitutional right to not talk to me.* This means that your forefathers, not your biological fathers, fought to give you this right. It is something you receive for being an American citizen and is to be respected and cherished. It does not mean you're guilty of not wanting to speak with me, no matter what I may say to you. *Anything you say to me at this point can and will be used against you in a court of law*. This means if you say something to me; you can't take it back, and say I didn't mean that, or that's not what I was trying to say. For, once you say it; I can twist it and bend it to make my case against you. This brings us to the next one. *You have a right*, here again—a right your forefathers fought and died for. This right says you can have *someone with you that understands the law*. Yep, actually went to school for it; didn't learn it in prison, and one that has experience with the games the cops are going to play with you. It's not a luxury, but a right. And the next one. *If you can't afford an attorney, then one will be appointed to you.* You definitely get what you pay for. That's all I have to say about that!

How does this fit with being a cop? I think somewhere along the line, we lost the ability to properly interact with the community we serve in. Yes, it is very easy to become tainted when dealing with the same negative situations over and over again; especially when you don't have the same issues at home.

STORY #18

For example, a troubled, bothersome couple lived in one of the areas in which I worked for some time. This couple—not sure they were actually a couple, but anyway. Most of the agency knew of them; whether they worked in the area where the couple lived, or not. Every night, the names of the couple would be blasted over the radio. Both of them had an alcohol problem. <u>*Who am I kidding? They were drunks.*</u> The man would do something and the woman would call for us to restore the behavior she wanted in the home. A few minutes later, it would be his turn. They would beat each other, and on and on it went. Both of them were arrested many times. For Pete's sake—the Judges even knew them by name! I had to respond to and deal with this type of behavior daily.

I had never seen anything like this growing up. The cops were never called to my home or my friend's homes. People didn't use the police as personal peacekeepers.

The fact is, there are a few of these people in every area of responsibility. Yes, the well-to-do, also. They call because so and so let their dog walk on my lawn while they were out walking it. Or, someone is sitting in the garage. I kid you not. What; I don't have a right to sit in the garage of the house I paid for? Or, the branches of his tree are hanging over into my yard. Really? People, get some sort of life! Yes, cops have to go on calls like this outside of very large, busy cities. I can just picture in my mind a call like this coming in on the south side of Chicago:

Dispatcher- "What's the nature of your call?"

Caller- "My neighbor was walking his dog and let it walk on my lawn."

Dispatcher- "And the dog attacked you."

Caller- "No, the dog just walked on my law, and I want you to send the police to tell him not to do it anymore."

Dispatcher- click....dial tone

Caller- "Hello, hello, is anyone there?"

Back to our story. On this particular night, the woman called again. She had already called four or five times. I responded to the home but just sat in my patrol car in their driveway. About five minutes had passed, when she must have called again because the dispatcher came over the radio asking if I was at the home. I didn't answer the dispatcher right away; which prompted him to repeat the transmission.

This time I replied, "Yes, I'm here."

I must have answered it in a strangely cold and distant way (You know, like when your last good nerve is so, so frazzled) because my sergeant came over the radio and said he would meet me there in a second. As I sat there, I started to think that maybe I should just go in there and choke the two of them and say I had found them that way. Because, the way they beat each other up; surely no one would question it.

I waited for the sergeant, who arrived shortly.

I KID YOU NOT; the sergeant got out of his car and said to me, "By the way you answered dispatch, I thought it might be best for me to show up to keep you from going in there and choking the two of them."

I replied, "Who, me? Sarge, No, I'm good."

What a liar! Now, what do you think my state of mind is going to be like in the next few minutes when I go to another call?— be professional, your feelings don't matter, bury your emotions and plug on.

THOUGHTS TO THINK ABOUT.

Many cops have to deal with similar situations during their shift. Think you can do it? That's why many have the bottle waiting for them when they get home. It all depends on the person and how they process all the STUFF! I have only personally known a few cops that had to drink every day to try and cope. For the most part, the ones I know are just social drinkers.

A decisive question for a cop to ask him/ herself when interviewing a suspect should be: "Is bullying this suspect into a confession the only way I can make this case?" If that's all the cop has, then it's not a very good case.

A difficult but very important question for the cop to ask him/herself is, "Does this person need to go to jail?"

One time a deputy told me that he tried to get at least one arrest every shift. Now, wait. Let's stop for a moment to examine where this point of view comes from before some of you blow a gasket and demand the name of the deputy so that he can be made to walk the plank. Cops are rewarded for the felony arrest they make. More arrest means a better chance at being promoted; few arrests— just what did you do all day?

Some cops will judge how good other cops are by the number of felony arrests they have made. Most new cops leave the academy aspiring to be— yep, Supper Cop. As we mature in job and person, we usually start to adjust that way of thinking.

When a cop really cares about the community in which he/she is serving, they desire to restore peace and order in the least intrusive way available—not like a bull in a china shop. However, when situations have festered and gotten out of hand, sometimes the bull in a china shop approach becomes necessary.

How do cops balance this? When do we arrest, and when do we find some other solution to quiet the problem? For, it can never be fixed by us.

Cops can only try to bring the community back to a somewhat manageable environment. Are you starting to see—many arrests make me Supper Cop, no arrest makes me a slug.

Many arrests within the community cause distrust of the police. While few arrests, if done for the right reason, normally equate to the community trusting the police. However, there is also a dangerous element to this approach. For if the cop becomes too forgiving, things will spiral out of control extremely fast. Thus, making the cop a community doormat. Cops go to work every day trying to juggle this!

Some white cops like to work in minority communities because of the possibility of making many felony arrests. (It's regrettable that we live in a time where everything needs a disclaimer. The reason I mention white here is that normally this work takes them into a community that is made up of a population that's different from what they are used to. Not always, but most of the time). And yes, black officers work in drug units, too. Ok?

There is usually no shortage of cops who want to work in the drug units. These cops need to be able to show the unit that they can do the job—right or wrong, it's a fact. I'm NOT saying that no drug arrest should be made—absolutely not. Narcotic use is out of control in all neighborhoods. It shows its ugly head one way within the inner cities and another way in the well-to-do neighborhoods. I can tell you this: it's much harder to get an arrest to stick with the well-to-do because their money buys really good lawyers. It's much easier in the inner city. Therefore, if I am a cop who wants to make a drug unit; which neighborhood do I want to work in? Rich people usually don't consent to anything of theirs being search by the United States Government. A cop has to do a lot more homework to make the case stick against the wealthy. On the other hand, the poor make it a little bit easier.

    I want my job performance graded on my ability to go on every call to service acting as if it's my own family that I'm responding to. Therefore, I try to be fair and impartial, looking for the least intrusive solution and not what might put sergeant stripes on my sleeve. And, yes, I know that many times family members need a kick in the Ass.

A cop's job is like no other. Irregularities are thrown at you every day. Throughout my career, I've said many times and also heard many other cops say many times, "Never seen that before?" Or, "That's a first!" After you've been on the job for some time and start to think that you've seen it all; some crazy new thing pops up out of nowhere.

We now live in a time where there is little respect shown to the men and women who wear the uniform. The older generation had respect for almost everything. It doesn't appear to be that way with the newer generation. It seems as if most of them believe they're owed something. Nowadays, cops come in contact with people who don't appear to respect anything. Many are people who only want what they want, and to hell with everyone else. If the cop doesn't placate them; they make a complaint against him/her in an attempt to get their way. This is very sad but true. I imagine the cops of the future will have to perform their duties void of all feelings and emotions. More like a robot. Despite all this; the brave men and women that wear a police uniform will put their lives on the line for whomever.

The pastor of the church I attend wanted to do sometime very special for all the first responders in our community. So, he came to me and asked for suggestions of things the church could do to honor and show appreciation for the first responders. He wanted it to be something that would be meaningful and very special to them.

I spoke with some of my colleagues about my pastor's request. Together we came up with the idea to design a challenge coin for every first responder in our county. I relayed this information back to my pastor and told him that I would design the coin for him.

Once the coin was designed, my pastor met with other local pastors to inquire if they wanted to participate in this special event for the first responders. So, my pastor and some other area pastors planned and organized the event.

Several pastors and their congregations joined with my pastor and his congregation to hold the special event to honor all the first responders of Indian River County. Every first responder of Indian River County received a challenge coin.

My colleagues and I want the citizens in our communities to know that we serve them because we care about them. So, a few of us composed *I Am My Brother's Keeper, the Cops Creed*. Below is a copy of the creed.

WHAT COPS WOULD LIKE YOU TO KNOW.

I Am My Brother's Keeper, the Cop's Creed

As law enforcement officials, we were made aware of, and have accepted the potential risks of keeping our communities safe. Make no mistake about it, we were informed, that at times, it would be an emotionally draining and thankless job. Nevertheless, if we are wearing the badge, it means we have agreed to the terms and conditions of this type of employment.

Many of you ask, "Knowing this, just why do you do this job?"

I can tell you, "It's not for the money, and I can assure you; we're qualified to do other things."

But, we do it because there's no peace in our souls when the innocent are being victimized or are in need.

We do it because when catastrophe strikes, our passion to help our neighbor overtakes us.

We do it to be able to look you square in the eye in the middle of chaos; reassuring you that it's going to be alright, and if not—then, it will be us who will pay the ultimate sacrifice, not you.

That day will come, and when it does, we promise you; we will not shrink back from our responsibility nor whine and complain asking, "Why me?" but we will charge forward aggressively, confronting whatever or whoever has come against our community.

And on that day, if our life is required, then it will not have been in vain. You see, our passing only confirms that the trumpet has sounded— calling us home. For, we know what awaits us on the other side.

And let it be known, that when we walk through those pearly gates, we will do so holding our heads up high with great pride. Only, to kneel before our Creator and thank Him for the honor to have been able to serve Him.

Now, you know why we do this job. For us, it's not a job. It's a calling.

We only ask one thing of you. Take care of our loved ones we leave behind. For, the fear they faced every day as they sent us off to work, has now come to pass.

It's not that we can when others can't, but that we will when others won't.

We are sure, and God knows we believe, that there are people from all different backgrounds and political affiliations, with many differences, but are willing to put those differences aside in times of trials to come together as one for the betterment of humanity.

And this act of compassion makes us refuse to believe we are a nation that is divided.

we refuse to believe that we have stopped caring about each other.

We refuse to believe that our interaction with each other cannot be understood or respected.

We refuse to believe that we are a nation that has forgotten how to have compassion

For, we know that what this nation is experiencing is nothing more than a speed bump, and soon shall pass.

If what we've been doing was going to work, then why hasn't it worked by now? Surely, we can't be the only ones thinking this.

So maybe, just maybe, it's time for us to get out of the way and put the responsibility back in our Creator's lap where it belongs—just a thought.

So, tonight, when we close our eyes; let us dream about continuing in this same spirit of unity. Let us quiet our minds and listen closely to what's in our hearts.

Let us reflect on what can be accomplished by doing this and then listen for that song.

Some of you may say, "What song?"

A song that will resonate in our hearts. A song that's not afraid to say, "I'm sorry, can we start over again?" A song that will usher in respect, compassion, and trust—a new song. A new song, that, when it's sung, will prepare a table of communion before us, despite all our differences. And this song will echo from east to west, from *north to south. Oh, what a glorious day that will be!*

That creed reflects the heart of a truly dedicated cop. I said heart, because I really believe that the good Lord chooses some of us to be his warriors here on earth. For, why is it that when disaster strikes we run to it and not away? Why is it that when my family has a business for me to go into? I declined and chose the uncertain world of law-enforcement? What makes me want to stop the bad from hurting the good? Who says to me each and every morning as I dress for work, "Don't screw this up, let's get it right."

What makes a cop say, "Out of all the things I could do in life, this is it?"

You can say what you please, but I believe it's a heavenly intervention. Since it's my book; that's what it is (smile). John 15:13 states, *"Greater love hath no man than this, that a man lay down his life for his friends."*

LET'S START TP WRAP THIS UP.

Some may wonder why I felt free to speak about some of my experiences that showed me in a somewhat negative light. I am so thankful to the good Lord that I've learned not to take myself too seriously. As a young man, I couldn't do this. The things I mentioned earlier in the book that I said I was thinking about doing—I would have done. Yep, and I would have had to suffer the consequence, too. However, with time, you start to season—so to speak.

One thing that I've learned to do very well is to say, "*I'm sorry*." Great power is in those two words. Those two words are doubly powerful when offered with an attitude of remorse. They can help turn a catastrophe into a pleasantry.

The ability to say, "*I'm sorry, can we start over again*" can heal many of the wrongs in some of our communities. I feel this should be taught in today's academies. Recruits must be taught the absolute power of this discipline. Why do I say discipline and not attitude? An attitude is a settled way of thinking or feeling about something or someone. Discipline is the PRACTICE of training. How a cop feels is immaterial at any given point and time, and is always going to fluctuate. A discipline must be practiced regularly to produce the desired results.

The United States Government should not take for granted the power it holds over its citizens. And this is exactly what the cop represents every time he/she interacts with the community. As a cop, I have the authority to take a life; which is a great responsibility. Using my career as an example—you see we don't always get it right. The cop will never, and I mean never, be able to detach himself/herself from belonging to the human race; meaning mistakes on any given day are the reality. Only a programmed robot would be immune to this.

The discipline of saying *"I'm sorry"* bypasses the conscious mind and instinctively comes out when mistakes are made. It will respond the same as any other discipline that has been taught to obtain good job performance. Cops shouldn't have to struggle with these two words. It should become an automatic response when a mistake of any kind is made. (Take a second and reflect on that again)

ALMOST FORGOT ABOUT THIS ONE.

A personal example of the *"I'm sorry, can we start over again"* discipline occurred one day in my assigned area. I was driving down a road when I spotted two young men forcing open a window and making entry into a home. The window was on the second floor. A covered porch provided a roof that enabled them access through the window.

As I drove up, one of the males saw me and just sat on the roof outside the window. The other male went into the home.

Some may say, surely this was proof that they belonged at the house because they didn't run away. Nope, it depends on the bad guy. Some have learned to act like they belong to deflect attention from what is really going on.

I pulled into the driveway and got out of the car. I approached the home and asked the young man that was sitting on the porch roof if I could speak with him. That's when all the fun started. The male began to tell me that he lived here, and I was just harassing him. I asked him to come down and show me something to prove to me he wasn't breaking into the home and did live there. He became agitated with me and called me a few choice words that I didn't even know existed.

I went on and said, "Look, man, *I'm sorry* for disrupting your day, but maybe you can possibly see it from my point of view? What happens if I just take your word for it and drive off; only to discover that you and your friend did break into this home?"

And I said, "Yes, your friend, for I saw him go through the window while I was driving up the block. It's not going to look good for me, and I don't think you would be happy with me if you discovered someone had broken into your home and I had seen the subjects doing it and I did nothing about it."

I then said, "How about this; I will give you any apology you want for having the police intrude into your afternoon if you will just comply with what I'm asking of you."

This guy made me say I was sorry a few times before he sent his friend out the front door with his driver's license which listed this address as his place of residence.

I said to him, "Come on, man, cut me some slack. Was that so hard? I'm not here to cause you any discomfort but am only trying to keep your home safe. And again, I apologize for any discomfort I may have caused you."

With that, the young man said, "We're cool."

I believe this same scenario was similar to the one that involved a professor that had been arrested for trying to get into his home. That incident caused President Obama to comment on it. I was not there, so I don't know all the particulars. However, my situation could have had a much different outcome had I not employed the *"I'm sorry, can we start over again"* discipline.

Driving off from the incident with the two young men on the porch roof, I thought that using the *"I'm sorry, can we start over again"* discipline shouldn't be so hard.

Some will say, "Doesn't that hurt—to eat mud?"

Not at all. The government can't afford to get it wrong and maintain the loyalty and trust of its citizens. Take a minute and think about it. You're home minding your own business, and now the police are all up in your business—makes you kind of go hmmm.

Using the *"I'm sorry, can we start over again"* discipline becomes hard when I have to look at a similar type of situation from a different set of eyes, and sometimes the eyes are foreign to me. This brings me to a tragic event that took place within our agency.

One of our deputies was visiting some of his family who resided in the same neighborhood where the shootings that I described earlier in this book had occurred. A block party of some sort was going on the evening of his visit. Many people had congregated out in the street.

Things went south when a confrontation developed between two rival wanna-be gangs. Shots were fired and one of the stray rounds struck and killed our deputy.

This senseless loss of life caused great empathy within this community and the Sheriff's Office. The family members, most of the community, and the Sheriff's Office desperately wanted whoever killed the deputy to be brought to justice.

Seeking justice for this horrific tragedy became complicated when no one, who had been present and had witnessed the tragedy, came forward with information. This lack of cooperation within the community set off a firestorm within the agency, and by all means, it should have. It should be simple, right? Whoever saw the person shoot the gun should come forward and give an eye-witness account so that justice can be served. No one came forward with information, for it seemed that no one had seen anything. Many people were interviewed, but all leads lead nowhere. No one wanted to put themselves on the line to be an eye-witness. This caused great frustration within the Sheriff's Office and parts of the community.

Some wondered what was the problem with the people in that community? Why didn't they speak up so the guilty ones could be apprehended? This point of view usually comes from a low crime community with no gang activity in it.

For the people in this community where the deputy was killed—it's a no-brainer. This type of community is very willing to help the police. When they see anything that looks like it could damage their community, they will call the police. They will go to court and testify because that is the only way a criminal can be brought to justice. They know where there is no eye-witness testimony, there is no conviction. Everyone knows the bad guy is not going to tell on himself. The citizens of the community know if the cops had been present when the shooting happened; they would have arrested the person involved. For then, they would be the ones to testify in court.

Similar situations play out in our inner-city communities. Most of the people who live in these communities are afraid of the gang element that populates them. These citizens are threatened all the time and told if anyone speaks up and gives the cops information, then they too will meet the same fate.

So, let's take a closer look at this. Some will say, "That's nonsense." For you and your environment, it probably is. This is a situation in which you would actually have to live in one of these communities to be able to speak about and to give a first-hand account of it. It is easy for us cops to get frustrated and ask the citizens of these communities what is their problem, and don't you want us to catch the bad guys who are running around destroying your community?

I think we cops take for granted that we belong to one of the largest gang on earth. In America, the membership is close to one million. No criminal enterprise has anywhere near this number of members. Notice I said criminal, not a terrorist.

Take a second and think about this. If someone hurts a cop, they will not only have that cop's agency looking for them but every agency in the world looking for them. So, just how many members is this? For example, if someone kills a cop in China, and the Chinese government discovers that this person is hiding out in an American city, and requests our assistance; we will be glad to oblige with the same tenacity as if that person had hurt one of our own.

At times, it's easy for cops to put pressure on citizens in a community to come forward and assist us with an investigation, for to take us on, you're going to have many others coming after you, no matter where you go.

I have personally told people, "I really need your help with this one, but if you choose not to help; I understand because the Sheriff's Office is not going to park a patrol car outside your home to keep you safe."

I say that because it"s right! That's the reason there is a witness protection program for high-profile cases. Unfortunately, most of these cases don't qualify for that program, and the people who live in these communities ain't stupid.

The train of thought in these situations is this: If I testify, what happens to me or my family in two, three, or six months from now? The police must work through this situation and try to come up with evidence of the crime that took place. In most cases, it's the eye-witness that is the missing element. Many crimes that happen in our inner-cities never get solved. That adds another tragedy for the victims' families.

Now, when something like this happens; the police start to operate in this big grey area. We need to catch this bad guy and the community is not assisting us. So, we usually apply a great amount of pressure on the community. In other words—If it moves, stop it. If it barks, shut it up. Zero tolerance is enforced.

The problem with this tactic is that many innocent bystanders will get caught up in this firestorm. In our tenacity to find the bad guy, sometimes it's easy to let our emotions get the best of us. At times the whole community can become the bad guy. Am I saying this tactic is wrong? Absolute not— unequivocally not. However, it needs to be conducted in a way that minimizes the negative consequences for the innocent.

At a time like this, the officers who have earned respect within the community should be called upon to take the lead. These officers know who most of the players are. These officers are the only ones who can minimize the negative effects of this type of operation. Notice how I said minimize, for there is no way that there will not be some causalities. They know the community leaders and business owners. They have proven themselves to be fair and impartial with their dealings in the community. These are the officers that always look for the least intrusive way to solve problems in the communities they serve. These officers are proficient in the discipline of *"I'm sorry, can we start over again?"*

When a community has to endure this type of pressure, whether it's justified or not, it creates a petri dish that breeds the Malcolm X's and Louis Farrakhan's of the world. Press on any community long and hard enough and fighters will be born. Yet, this same petri dish was also responsible for the birth of the great prophet of peace, Dr. Martin Luther King. (Dear, Lord, will there ever be another?)

Read my lips. I am NOT saying that pressure should not be placed where many of the senseless deaths are taking place—absolute not, but the innocent must be taken into account. If an agency doesn't have officers proficient in the discipline of *"I'm sorry, can we start over again?"*; it's going to be a long and hard investigation. Once a situation becomes heated, this is the only discipline that will be embraced by the community to allow the pressure to be applied where needed; thus, minimizing the casualties.

Conclusion

When I was seventeen years old, I had a 1968 Roadrunner. The car had different color primer spots all over it to prepare the body for a paint job—a high school auto shop thing. It was a hotrod with big tires and loud mufflers. It was different than the other cars on the road.

One day my fifteen years old friend and I were going to a special hotrod shop that was two towns away. At that time big afros were the thing, and both of us had them—gigantic Michael Jackson afros. So, we were cruising along obeying the speed limit. I made sure I obeyed the speed limit because the cops were always looking for reasons to stop vehicles in this town. The windows were down and my music was playing. Yes, it was an eight-track tape.

Then, I was pulled over. My friend went into the glove box to turn off the music because that is where most people put their eight tracks if you didn't want to have them stolen. As he reached to turn off the music, the cops came over a loudspeaker shouting for us to stop what we were doing and stick our hands out the window. I knew what is going on because I heard stories from one of my cop uncles. He had told me about felony stops, and guess what—now I found myself in one.

I had never been in any trouble outside of the occasional speeding ticket, or two, or three, and here my friend and I are now being ordered out of the vehicle at gunpoint! Two of the cops had shotguns pointed at us.

We were in the middle of the street, sprawled out, face down on the road. The cops had shut down both lanes of travel, and all attention was on us. While we are lying face down in the road, some of the cops began to search my car and the others kept us at gunpoint. No permission to search was asked.

At that point in time, I hadn't the foggiest clue as to why we had been stopped. No one had told us anything except to put our hands out the window, back out of the car, and lay face down to the ground. Every time I tried to ask a question; I was ordered to shut up! My fifteen years old friend was freaking out, and both of us were hoping that none of the cops shot us!

After what seemed like an eternity, the cops said we could go—just like that. No explanation. Nothing. I became agitated and asked what did we do? One of the cops said my vehicle fit the description of one used in a robbery. I knew this could not have been true because my vehicle was very unique looking, due to the many different colors on it from the bodywork that was being done.

I told the cops that they were a bunch of liars because my car doesn't look like anything else on the road. Look at it! Then, I asked if they were going to put my car back together again? They all just laughed at me and said, yea, right!

They had literally torn my car apart. Whatever could be ripped off was laying out in the street. I yelled at them and said that my uncle was a cop in the next town over and that I would be telling him about this. My friend was pleading for me to shut up before we caught a beating.

We had to retrieve all the guts of my vehicle that were in the road; with no assistance from the cops. We darted in and out of traffic to collect the items that had been thrown out into the road. That whole event was very frightening as well as extremely embarrassing—dancing in and out of traffic trying to get your stuff with people trying to run over you.

I have never forgotten it. The memory is seared in my mind. When I became a cop, I vowed to never treat anyone like that. My point in sharing this experience is to emphasize the importance of the *"I'm sorry, can we start over again?"* discipline is much easier to develop if you have personally experienced similar trauma.

The Parable of the Two Wolves

An old Cherokee is teaching his grandson about life. A fight is going on inside of me, he said to the little boy.

It's a terrible fight and it's between two wolves. One is evil-he is anger, envy, sorrow, regret, greed, arrogance, self-pity, guilt, resentment, inferiority, lies, false pride, superiority, and ego.

The other is good-he is joy, peace, love, hope, serenity, humility, kindness, benevolence, empathy, generosity, truth, compassion, and faith. The same fight is going on inside of you, and inside every other person, too.

The grandson thought about it for a minute and then asked his grandfather, "Which wolf will win?"

The old Cherokee simply replied, "The one you feed."

People tend to navigate towards one or the other wolf inside them. Most people move toward the good wolf. The ones who live for destruction move toward the bad. A cop is made up of both. He must have enough of the bad wolf to have the tenacity to enter the fight. But, enough of the good wolf to know when, how, and what to fight.

Some people, on this earth, are hell-bent on causing pain and destruction. Thus, they live for the fight. Yet, most people, when threatened, never consider getting into the fight.

Cops fully understand this about human nature and take on the responsibility of protecting the ones who want nothing to do with the fight. I think Dr. Martin Luther King and Philosopher Hegel described it best, *"Not ordinarily do men achieve this balance of opposites. The idealists are not usually idealistic. The militant are not generally known to be passive, nor the passive to be militant. Seldom are the humble self-assertive, or the self-assertive humble. ...Truth is found neither in the thesis nor the antithesis, but in an emergent synthesis that reconciles the two."*

Dr. Martin Luther King's <u>I Have A Dream</u> speech ranks number one on the top one hundred American speeches of the 20th Century. He was awarded five honorary degrees and at the age of thirty-five was the youngest man to have ever received the Nobel Peace Prize. His ability to clearly articulate the song that was in his heart is a modern-day masterpiece. His ability to stimulate conviction, while maintaining benevolence, was truly masterful. For, out of his mouth came a sword that demanded equality and justice for all. The cure for the ills of the inner cities can be found in the writings of this man. And the police can find a fresh perspective for the inner-cities in Dr. King's writings. I speak from experience. For this is where I discovered the discipline of "*I'm sorry, can we start over again*?"

For the general public, it is my desire that this book has shed light on just what it's like to be a cop. And for the cops, to take some time to reflect on, and truly realize your enormous responsibility, and never forget you're there to serve the Creator, by protecting His creation.

The end.

Made in the USA
Columbia, SC
18 May 2022